DICK WHITTINGTON

OR

LOVE IS THE KEY THAT OPENS EVERY DOOR

by

V. C. CLINTON-BADDELEY

With music by
GAVIN GORDON

LONDON

SAMUEL FRENCH LIMITED

For Amateur Production Enquiries

United Kingdom and World
EXCLUDING NORTH AMERICA
plays@samuelfrench.co.uk
020 7255 4302/01

Each title is subject to availability from Samuel French,
depending upon country of performance.

CHARACTERS

Fairy Snowflake
Simon
Sally
Marmaduke Bung
Alderman Bung
Alderman Fitzwarren
Dame Cicely Suett
Dick Whittington
The Cat
Alice Fitzwarren
King Rat
An Elderly Citizen
1st Sailor
2nd Sailor
3rd Sailor
4th Sailor
The Mate
Ship's Cook
Neptune
Britannia
Sultan
Chief Eunuch
Master of the Household
Warder
Chorus, Apprentices, Sea Creatures, Mermen, Sea Nymphs, Girls of the Harem, Court Officials, White Cat etc.

SYNOPSIS OF SCENES

PROLOGUE

Before a Front Cloth

ACT I

ACT II

ACT III

PROLOGUE   Before a Front Cloth

SCHEDULE OF MUSIC

AUTHOR'S NOTE

THIS version of *Dick Whittington* was written with the joint
encouragement of the Bristol Old Vic company and of the Esso
Music and Drama Group, Fawley, Hampshire. It was produced
at the Theatre Royal, Bristol, on the 22nd December, 1955, and
shortly afterwards at Fawley in January, 1956.

PROLOGUE

1. "PRELUDE" (CHORUS)

Off stage voices are heard singing "Turn again, Whittington, thou worthy citizen, Lord Mayor of London", as the curtain rises on a prologue cloth. Enter FAIRY SNOWFLAKE *from the* R.

SNOWFLAKE.
　　So there you are, my dears! Yet once again
　　The year revolves and Christmas comes to reign,
　　And here, as ever at this festive hour,
　　Comes Fairy Snowflake with her magic power.
　　Too often, as you know, at just this time
　　Some goblin seeks to spoil our pantomime,
　　By plotting discord and with laughter rude
　　Scoffing at Love and moral rectitude.
　　But *this* year seems to mark a disappearance
　　Of all this diabolic interference—
　　And I am hoping there may be no call
　　To use my necromantic art at all:
　　For young Dick Whittington is such a lad—
　　Incapable, my dears, of being bad:
　　Upright in spirit, sound in heart and limb,
　　I think no fiend will get the best of *him*.
　　Besides—I've scanned the heavens: it seems to me,
　　With Jupiter in the ascendancy,
　　And Venus, favourite influence of the sky,
　　Uprising in the sign of Gemini,
　　No evil chance can possibly destroy
　　The rosy fortune of my favourite boy.
　　And so, methinks, with little cause for fear
　　We open our festivity this year,
　　Intent to trace Dick Whittington's romance
　　Through a superb mosaic of song and dance.
　　　　Have a good time my dears!—but none the less,
　　Be on your guard against licentiousness!
　　One never knows . . . and *should* aught supervene
　　To mar the tranquil beauty of our scene,
　　Remember this year's moral I implore
　　"Love is the key that opens every door!"

(A soft music begins. The lights fade down, leaving only a spot upon Fairy Snowflake)

1

But lo! The labyrinths of Time and Space
Dissolve beneath the spell of Love's embrace—
And magic hands draw back the veil to show
Springtime in England many years ago.

(*Bells are heard in the music*)

Hark! The brave bells of Bow with merry chime
Ring up the curtain on our pantomime,
While willing 'prentices, the streets adorning,
Walk happily to work this bright May morning.

(*Exit* FAIRY SNOWFLAKE *as the prologue cloth rises and the lights
snap up on the opening chorus*)

ACT I

SCENE 1

SCENE—*The city of London on a May morning in 1380—or somewhere about then.*

On the L *is the timbered front of* ALDERMAN FITZWARREN'S *drapery establishment. On the other side is the house of* ALDERMAN BUNG, *a brewer. It will be useful if there can be two steps up to the front door of* BUNG'S *house. At the back of the stage wide steps lead up to a raised footway protected with posts and chains. Beyond, a prospect of London streets and houses stretches into the distance.*

When the CURTAIN *rises enter London apprentices of a variety of trades— including* SIMON, *Fitzwarren's apprentice, and* SALLY, *his maid- servant—on their way to work.*

2. "OPENING CHORUS" (CHORUS)

ALL.

Ding-dong,
Ding-ding,
The steeples ring,
On holidays
A merry thing—
But not so gay
When belfries say
It's time to start
A working day.

For what are early bells to we
But hideous cacophony,
As off to work, with weary yawn,
'Prentices plod at crack of dawn.

We all
Concur,
Without demur,
From Baker down
To Shoemaker,
That bells that tong,
Ding-dong, ding-dong,
At break of day
Are wholly wrong.

MEN.

Ding Dong, Ding Dong
It's time to start a working day.

Girls.

Tingaling, Tingaling
Ding-Dong bell
Tingaling, Tingaling
Ding-Dong bell.

All.

But London-born apprentices
Must rise above such weaknesses,
And strive to catch the worm we've heard
Always awaits the early bird.

So make
A stir,
Upholsterer,
The Weaver and
The Fishmonger
And Milkmaid sing
Like anything——
And so to work
With ding-dong-ding.

Girls.

Tingaling, Tingaling
Ding-Dong bell
Tingaling, Tingaling
Ding-Dong bell.

Men.

Ding-Dong, Ding-Dong
It's time to start a working day.

(*During the dance that follows* Marmaduke Bung *enters and gets entangled and deliberately ragged. Exeunt* Apprentices *to a repeat of* "So make a stir" *etc.* Alderman Bung *and* Alderman Fitzwarren *enter from their two houses*)

Marmaduke. Oh! Oh!

Bung. Rogues! Vagabonds! This is disgraceful. Are you hurt, my son?

Marmaduke. I think not, Father.

Bung. Heaven be praised!

Marmaduke. But I fear my doublet must be quite spoiled.

Bung. I shall complain to the Lord Mayor. Do you support me, Alderman Fitzwarren?

Fitzwarren. Well, Alderman Bung—we must make allowances. Youth, sir, must have its fling.

Marmaduke. They flung me on the ground. And what waste of time, sir, dancing in the streets like that. Think of all the valuable working hours lost. I hope, sir, they will all be at their tasks tomorrow at four in the morning to make up for it.

Bung. You see, sir—my son has a good head for business. He knows what's what, sir; he will make a worthy companion to your charming daughter, Master Fitzwarren.

Fitzwarren. Ah yes, Master Bung, I was forgetting. We have business together. Shall we proceed, sir?

Bung. Certainly, sir. We await your pleasure.

Fitzwarren. I will first acquaint Dame Suett of my whereabouts, sir, and then I will attend you. (*He knocks on the door, opens it and calls out*) "Cicely!"

(*Enter at the door* Cicely Suett, *the Alderman's Cook, dressed in costume of a modern cook, neatly aproned, sleeves turned up, hands and arms covered in flour, and brandishing a rolling pin*)

Cicely. Now what is it, Master Fitzwarren, out with it, if you please, because I'm in the middle of making an apple pie. It's always the same with you. No sooner start on something than I'm called away, and then you wonder why it is I get muddled and put your gloves in the boiled batter pudding last Sunday. Mistakes will happen.

Fitzwarren. Certainly, certainly.

Cicely. We can't help mistakes, I say. We *are* human—or some of us are. Now what is it this time? I can't stand here all day, talking, you know.

Fitzwarren. Well, Cicely, I only wanted to ask you to tell Miss Alice——

Cicely. Miss Alice is out——

Fitzwarren. I know that, Cicely.

Cicely. Well, how d'you expect me to tell her?

Fitzwarren. When she comes *in*, Cicely, when she comes *in*.

Cicely. Oh, I see—that's different—when she comes in—why didn't you say so at first?

Fitzwarren. Inform Miss Alice that I am over at Alderman Bung's house, negotiating a little business, and ask her if she will prepare some spiced ale for us in the parlour. We shall return presently. Just tell her that Cicely. Now, sir.

(*The three men begin to cross towards the other house*)

Bung. The papers are all waiting, Master Fitzwarren. It will be a proud moment for my son, sir—will it not, Marmaduke?

Marmaduke. Oh, yes, sir; precisely, sir; a proud moment is just what it will be; that is the very thing I was going to say.

(*The men disappear into Alderman Bung's house, and* Cicely *advances to confer with the audience*)

Cicely. There they go with their papers and their proud moments. But they can't fool me. I can see what it is. Master Fitzwarren is after the money bags and he's going to marry

Miss Alice to that spindle-shanked egg-faced, half-cooked pancake, Marmaduke Bung. She that I've known since she was no bigger than my rolling pin, the poor lamb. It's a shame, that's what it is. Still, you can't force a girl to marry. Perhaps she'll say no. That's what I've always said.

3. "Cupboard Love" (Cicely)

I

Cicely.

> If a girl sets her target too low—o
> 　She'll always have cause to complain
> And therefore I've always said "No—o"
> 　For reasons judicious and sane.
> The fellows who praise up my beauty
> 　Betray what they mean with one look:
> It isn't Dan Cupid that makes them so stupid—
> 　They want me because I can cook . . .
>
> Cupboard Love!
> 　Such is my fate.
> Cupboard Love—
> 　What's on the plate?
> When will a gentleman
> When will a gentleman
> 　Love me for only me?

II*

> When they woo me with masculine ardour
> 　I see through their impudent lies—
> They're really in love with my larder
> 　They just want my puddings and pies.
> When they talk of my lovely proportions
> 　I know where their ecstasies point:
> It isn't my figure they praise with such vigour—
> 　They don't need a wife but a joint!
>
> Cupboard Love!
> 　Such is my fate.
> Cupboard Love—
> 　What's on the plate?
> When will a gentleman
> When will a gentleman
> 　Love me for only me?

III

> But when I find my true love I'll show him
> 　The perfectly blissful receipt—

* Verse 2 can be cut if necessary.

> Take two hearts and mix to a poem
> And bring to a very great heat.
> Add kisses, and sugar, and money,
> In equal proportions all three—
> Now—who's going through it with Cicely Suett?
> Oh! Who'll make a soufflé with me?

Eh? Any offers?

(*The* Cat *bounds on down the steps and rubs himself affectionately against* Cicely's *legs. She shrugs her shoulders*)

See what I mean?
> Cupboard Love!
> Such is my fate!
> Cupboard Love—
> What's on the plate?
> When will a gentleman
> When will a gentleman
> Love me for only me?

(Cicely Suett *enters the house, the* Cat *follows. A moment later* Cicely *is heard shouting and the* Cat *leaps out with a fish in its mouth. Enter* Dick *along the raised walk at the back*)

Dick. Puss! Puss! There you are—and you've got something for breakfast:

(*The* Cat *points to the house*)

You asked for it, I suppose?

(*The* Cat *assents*)

I thought so. If *I* ask I'm a beggar, a rogue, a vagabond—but if *you* ask, you're just a sweet, sweet, pussy cat.

(*The* Cat *rolls at his feet*)

And so you are—so you are. But what am *I* going to have for breakfast, eh?

(Dick *sits down on Alderman Bung's steps*)

> Far have we wandered, Pussy, you and I,
> Through woods and lanes beneath the April sky,
> Led on by fairy voices in the air
> That whispered we should find our fortunes here.
> Our fortunes, Puss! Why were we ever told
> That London's streets were paved with solid gold?
> We've met no kindly faces—not a friend
> To give us welcome here at journey's end.

Has Fate contrived to lead us to this place
Only to offer hunger and disgrace?
I'll not believe it on this golden day—
Something—or someone—sweet must come my way.

(*Along the raised walk, down the steps, and down the stage towards her house comes* ALICE FITZWARREN. *The* CAT *bounds across the stage and rubs against her leg*)

CAT. Maiow!
ALICE. Why, what a darling lovely cat! Where did you come from, Pussy?
DICK (*who has followed the Cat*) He's mine, Miss.
ALICE. Oh! I did not see you, sir.
DICK. I'm sorry, Miss, if I startled you.
ALICE. It is no matter, sir. I was surprised to see anyone. Most people are at work by this hour.
DICK. We have only just arrived, Miss. From the country. We've come to seek our fortunes, Miss.
ALICE. I hope you will find them, sir.
DICK. I hope so, Miss; but it is all very bewildering at first. Do you know—could you advise me, Miss?—where I might best apply for work?
ALICE. There are many fine businesses about, sir. I doubt not but that there may be opportunities in some of them—perhaps at Alderman Fitzwarren's.
DICK. Oh, thank you, Miss.
ALICE. You will succeed I am sure—especially with this lovely cat to help you.
CAT. Miaow!

(*A church chime strikes the half hour*)

ALICE. Alas! How quickly the time goes. I should be home by this.
DICK. Can you not stay a little, Miss? It is early yet.
ALICE. I wish I might, sir . . . but, no, it is impossible. I must go. I wish you good day, sir, and good fortune.
DICK. Thank you, Miss.

(*Exit* ALICE *into Alderman Fitzwarren's house. She drops her purse as she goes.* DICK *strides across the stage in romantic ecstasy. The* CAT *investigates the purse*)

DICK.
　　O fairest fate! Now all my life seems clear—
　　This was the star that drew my footsteps here!

(*The* CAT *bounds across and taps him with his paw*)

　　Don't interrupt, Puss, when I'm speaking verse.
CAT. Wow!

Dick.   What's the matter?
Cat.   Wow!
Dick.   What's this? A purse!

Her purse! A blessing on your clever paw!
This is the key unlocks my lady's door.
(*He strides across to the Fitzwarren doorway*)
Look out for larks! He who would pluck a rose
Must have a heart for danger—so here goes!

(Dick *knocks on the door. On the instant* Alderman Bung's *door opens and out comes* Bung, Marmaduke *and* Fitzwarren)

Fitzwarren (*approaching*) Young man—why are you knocking at my door?

(Alice *appears at the Fitzwarren door*)

Dick. This purse, sir. It was dropped just now by a young lady —this young lady, sir—and I wanted to return it.
Alice (*receiving it*) Oh, thank you, sir.
Fitzwarren. H'm . . . Well, young man, my daughter and I are grateful to you . . .
Alice. Yes, indeed.
Fitzwarren. And I suppose you must have a reward. Here is a penny.
Dick. Thank you, sir, very much—but I don't want a reward. I won't take money, sir.
Fitzwarren. Not want a reward? Such honesty overwhelms me.
Marmaduke. I never heard anything like it.
Fitzwarren. Can I do nothing for you, young man?
Dick. Yes, sir, there is something. I want work.
Fitzwarren. Work?
Bung. Work!
Marmaduke. Did he say *work*?
Fitzwarren. This is the most remarkable case I ever met with, Alderman Bung. He actually wants work. What is your name, young man?
Dick. Dick Whittington, sir.
Fitzwarren. Well, Whittington, I applaud your resolution and, um . . .
Alice. Dear Father!
Fitzwarren. Yes, Alice.
Alice. The lad looks well favoured and honest. Could you not offer him an apprenticeship in your own business?
Dick. If you only would, sir! I promise I would work hard.
Bung. Is this wise, Alderman Fitzwarren?
Marmaduke. Consider, sir; he may be a footpad.
Bung. He has an extraordinary cast of feature. I would be slow to trust him myself.

B

FITZWARREN. Upon my word——

ALICE. Oh, *do*, Father!

FITZWARREN. Well, Alice child, you may be right. You have a good judgement. Young man—if you are willing to enter my service I will take you.

DICK. Thank you, sir.

FITZWARREN. You will, of course, receive no payment during your seven years' apprenticeship—but you will have a good bed under the counter and good meals with your fellows. Do you agree to that?

DICK. I shall consider myself well paid, sir, to be a member of your household.

FITZWARREN. Very well. If you will bring your possessions this evening, Dame Suett will receive you. Come, Alderman Bung.

BUNG (*following to enter the house*) I think you are very rash, Alderman Fitzwarren. Very rash indeed, sir.

MARMADUKE. I only hope you may not all be murdered in your beds. A slippery fellow he seems to me.

(*Exeunt* BUNG, FITZWARREN *and* MARMADUKE. ALICE *lingers by the door*)

DICK. Then you are Mistress Fitzwarren, Miss?

ALICE. Yes, sir.

DICK. You did not say so when you suggested that I should apply for work here.

ALICE. No, sir . . . it seemed so bold . . . but I hoped you would follow my advice.

DICK. Oh, Miss—how can I thank you for your kindness?

ALICE. By working well, sir . . . and justifying my confidence.

FITZWARREN (*off*) Alice!

ALICE. Yes, Father! . . . Good-bye . . .

FITZWARREN (*off*) Come hither, child!

DICK. . . . Till we meet again! . . .

(*Exit* ALICE)

. . . Till we meet again. Oh, Puss! We've done it! We're in! And it was all your idea!

CAT. Maiow!

DICK. Nothing can stop us now. We're on the road!

4. "LONDON IS NOT PAVED WITH GOLD"
(DICK and CHORUS)

I

DICK.
    London is not paved with gold
      That's an old wives' story—
    Yet it's true that London streets
      Lead to fame and glory.

London bells just ring ding-dong
    In their normal function—
But to me they sing a song
    Of discreet injunction:

(*The* Chorus, *led by* Simon *and* Sally, *attracted by the song, come softly on and gather round Dick inquisitively. Gradually they join in*)

Chorus

Put your best foot forward, hold your head up high,
    March on the crown of the road!
Leave the ditches to the dunderheads and stride straight on
    Should'ring a pack well stowed.
Follow my way, that's the best way, not the by-way,
    Stick to the Highway Code—
If you're careful round the bend
You will get there in the end
Down the great Big Business Road.

II

Dick.
Nose in ledgers, chained to desk,
    Hearts on dusty shelves,
Few can point the way to take,
    Strangers here themselves.
London bells just ring ding-dong
    Where there's no ambition:
I can hear their secret song
    Full of admonition—
Chorus.
Put your best foot forward, hold your head up high,
    March on the crown of the road!
Leave the ditches to the dunderheads and stride straight on
    Shouldering a pack well stowed.
Follow my way, that's the best way, not the by-way,
    Stick to the Highway Code—
If you're careful round the bend
You will get there in the end
Down the great Big Business Road.

Simon. Well, sir, we've all enjoyed ourselves very much and I'm sure we're much obliged to you for giving us a lead—but might we make so bold as to ask who you be and why you're a'making of all this celebrating.
Dick. Yes, friend. My name is Dick Whittington, and this is my cat.
Chorus. Lumme!

Dick. And I'm celebrating because Alderman Fitzwarren has engaged me as his apprentice.

Simon. Has he now? Well, I'm another. And all the rest of the boys is apprenticed to someone and the girls is all milkmaids—except Sally, and she's Miss Alice's maid—and my name's Simon.

Dick. God save you, friends!

Chorus. And you, Dick!

Dick. So we'll be working together.

Simon. You never said a truer word.

Sally. Up with the lark!

1st Girl. Scrubbing!

1st Man. Cleaning!

2nd Girl. Milking!

2nd Man. Polishing!

Sally. Undoing stock——

Simon. Doing it up again——

Sally. Counting——

Simon. Running messages——

Sally. Never a minute's rest!

1st Girl. It's terrible.

2nd Girl. It's dreadful.

Simon. It's perishing awful.

Dick. I don't mind hard work. You must work hard if you're going to make a fortune——

1st Man. Make a fortune!

2nd Man. *What* did you say?

Simon. My poor fellow-labourer, you don't understand. Apprentices don't make fortunes.

Chorus. No.

Simon. They just work.

Chorus. Yes.

5. "A 'Prentice I Would Be"

(Simon, Dick and Chorus)

I

Simon.

> The world of commerce, fellow slave,
> Is not what you suppose.
>> However hard you sweat and toil
>> You'll get no portion of the spoil
> As everybody knows.

All.

> As everybody knows.

Dick.

> But a 'prentice I would be!

All.

> Yes, a 'prentice he would be!

II

ALL.

> To grind the faces of the poor
> Was once our earnest aim,
>   But, after years a 'prentice bound,
>   Ambition falters to the ground,
> And yours will do the same,
> And yours will do the same.

DICK.

> But a 'prentice I would be!

ALL.

> Yes, a 'prentice he would be!

III

SIMON.

> Be warned in time, my likely lad,
>   A 'prentice is not free.
> Tormented, starved, chastised, oppressed,
> You'll go the way of all the rest,
> And end up just like me—

ALL.

> And end up just like me.

DICK.

> But a 'prentice I would be!

ALL.

> Yes, a 'prentice he would be!

IV

ALL.

> But if, in spite of all advice,
>   To join us you intend,
> Don't be too anxious for your fate—
> We might, perhaps, exaggerate,
>   At least you'll make good friends,
>   At least you'll make good friends.

DICK.

> So—a 'prentice I shall be!—
> Yes—a 'prentice he shall be!—

SCENE 2

SCENE—*A London street.*

6. *Entrance of* KING RAT

Enter KING RAT, L. *He is the conventional demon-king in scarlet tights with rat ears: and he is looking uncommonly crafty.*

KING RAT.
    Hush! Not a sound! In every Christmas play
    The Powers of Darkness give themselves away,
    Revealing all too soon what they are after
    By premature and loud satanic laughter.
    Time and again I've seen some demon make
    The very same ridiculous mistake—
    His stratagems betrayed and nothing worth
    All for one blast of ill-considered mirth.
    But *this* year—sssh! King Rat intends to see
    That things are managed more efficiently . . .
    This Whittington—vile Snowflake's latest brat
    Makes a companion of a monstrous cat,
    The Prince of Mousers and acknowledged ace
    In every combat with the rodent race.
    My task it is, and my supreme delight,
    To lure this creature to a mortal fight,
    And wreak on him and on his priggish master
    Appalling vengeance and condign disaster.
    Haha!— But sssh! King Rat must do his worst
    To choke his laughter though his sides should burst—
    And by this fiendish act of abnegation
    Bring Snowflake, Dick and Cat, to desolation.

"SONG OF KING RAT" (KING RAT)

Till the dirty work be done
I must curb my sense of fun.
All may be
Black depravity—
But not a single laugh from me.
Ha-ha! Ha-ha! Shush! Shush!
But not a single laugh from me.

When the victory is mine
I shall laugh like other swine—
Once again
Bellow like a drain—
But now my laughter I restrain,
From filthy motives,
Yes, now my laughter I restrain.

(*Exit* KING RAT)

SCENE 3

SCENE—*Interior of Alderman Fitzwarren's shop.*
    *A counter, with bales of cloth, tape-measures, outsize tailor's shears,
runs parallel with the* L *wall. The back cloth represents shelves and
goods. By the middle of the right-hand wall is Fitzwarren's safe. The*

downstage L *entrance is the communicating door to the private house.
The upstage* R *entrance is the shop door to the street. Enter from house
entrance* SALLY *with a bucket and scrubbing brush,* SIMON *with a mop,
and* DAME SUETT *with a dustpan and brush.*

7. "WHO'LL SCRUB THE DOORSTEP"

(CICELY, SALLY and SIMON)

I

ALL.

Who'll scrub the doorstep,
the doorstep,
the doorstep,
Who'll scrub the doorstep
And wash the dirt away?

SALLY.

I'll scrub the doorstep,
the doorstep,
the doorstep,

ALL.

I'll }
He'll } scrub the doorstep
And wash the dirt away.

II

ALL.

Who'll mop the lino,
the lino,
the lino,
Who'll mop the lino
And wash the dirt away?

SIMON.

I'll mop the lino,
the lino,
the lino,

ALL.

I'll }
He'll } mop the lino
And wash the dirt away.

III

ALL.

Who'll sweep the carpet,
the carpet,
the carpet,
Who'll sweep the carpet
And brush the dirt away?

CICELY.

> I'll sweep the carpet,
>> the carpet,
>> the carpet,

ALL.

> I'll ⎫
> She'll ⎭ sweep the carpet
> And brush the dirt away.

SIMON. Oh—Dame Suett, couldn't we use the carpet sweeper?

SALLY. Oh—please, Dame Suett—just this once. Do let's! No dust!

SIMON. No unpleasant odour.

SALLY. Satisfaction guaranteed.

SIMON. Or money returned.

SALLY. That's what it says, Dame Suett. Couldn't we?

SIMON. For a treat, Ma'am?

CICELY. Well, you know what I think of the dratted things. Carpet sweepers indeed! Usually the flint won't work, or the gunpowder's wet. One or the other. But it's just like Master Fitzwarren. Must be up-to-date. The French Ambassador has one —so he has to have one, too.

SIMON. But I've been over it, Ma'am. I think it will work all right today.

CICELY. Very well, then.

SIMON. Oh, thank you, Dame Suett.

(*Exit* SIMON)

CICELY. What I say is, give me the old dustpan and brush— and that's what it usually comes to.

(*Re-enter* SIMON *with a contraption vaguely like a Hoover, involving all sorts of pulleys and strings and a propeller like a helicopter above*)

SIMON. There you are, Ma'am.

CICELY. Very well, Simon, strike a flint and see what you can do.

(*A chugging noise, reinforced from the wings, follows;* SIMON *turns a handle and everything starts to revolve*)

SIMON. There you are!

(*The contraption starts to move,* SIMON *directing it like a lawn mower. Suddenly it gets out of hand. The noise increases and it starts rushing about, chasing* SALLY *and* DAME SUETT *all over the shop.* Finally there is an explosion and a cloud of smoke. All three are in various positions of prostration when* ALDERMAN FITZWARREN *enters with* DICK. SALLY *goes out*)

* In the Bristol production much was made of this business and additional dialogue written. It is a production matter.

FITZWARREN. Ah! There you are, Dame Suett—hard at it, I see.

CICELY. Here I am, Master Fitzwarren, and I should like to remind you that I was engaged to dress the dinner and not to do the housework. Just look at me, I ask you, and me the best cook in Cheapside.

FITZWARREN. Cicely! Cicely! My good soul!

CICELY. Don't you good soul me, Master Fitzwarren.

FITZWARREN. I have just come here, Cicely, to introduce my new apprentice, Dick Whittington. Now, with his help, Cicely, we shan't have to ask you to do so much.

CICELY. Well—that's something.

FITZWARREN. Now, Dick—this is Dame Suett, my trusted housekeeper.

DICK. Good day, Ma'am.

FITZWARREN. This is Simon, your fellow-apprentice—and this, Dick, is the shop.

DICK. Yes, sir.

FITZWARREN. And here is the safe—with all my takings in it, for a week, Dick. (*He opens the door*) I must presently to the bankers, and you shall accompany me.

(*Enter* SALLY)

SALLY. If you please, Master, the Lord Mayor is in the parlour and will be glad if you will wait upon him, sir.

(*Exit* SALLY)

FITZWARREN. The Lord Mayor! Great goodness! This may bode well for business. Dick, I will return to you later.

DICK. Yes, sir.

FITZWARREN. Meantime, Dame Suett and Simon, will you teach the lad his business. The Lord Mayor! Bless my soul! This may have important consequences.

(*Exit* FITZWARREN)

CICELY. H'm—so you want to learn the business, eh? †

DICK. Yes, please, Dame Suett.

CICELY. Well, there's only one rule, isn't there, Simon?

SIMON. That's right, Dame Suett.

DICK. What is it, Ma'am?

CICELY. "The customer is always right". That's the rule, Dick. It will get you anywhere.

DICK. It doesn't seem a very helpful one.

CICELY. Ha! He doesn't understand, Simon.

† The following scene was cut at Bristol to compensate for the length of time expended on the cleaning machine. But it would be possible to include both or to cut the machine and concentrate on "the citizen scene". Both are traditional jokes.

Simon. No, Dame Suett.

Cicely. We must learn him.

Simon. Yes, Dame Suett. Here's a customer coming now, Dame Suett.

Cicely. A customer! The very thing! You stand here, Dick, and watch me and Simon deal with him.

(Cicely *and* Simon *take their places behind the counter*)

And remember the watchword—"The customer is always right".

(*Enter, from the street, an elderly and crusty citizen—or it could be* Alderman Bung *himself*)

Good morning, sir. Nice bright morning.

Citizen. Chilly.

Cicely. Well, yes, sir, there is a touch of North wind.

Citizen. East.

Cicely. East, is it, sir? They are both cold winds.

Citizen. East is colder.

Cicely. Yes, sir, of course. And what can we do for you, sir?

Citizen. I want some cloth——

Cicely. Yes, sir: cloth for a cloak?

Citizen. For a coat. And nothing expensive.

Cicely. Now what colour, sir? We have a handsome green.

Citizen. Blue.

Cicely. Blue, sir? Much more suitable. Now here, sir, is an excellent blue——

Citizen. How much?

Cicely. Five groats the yard, sir.

Citizen. Too expensive.

Cicely. It *is* expensive, sir——

Citizen. Then why d'you show it to me?

Cicely. I can't think—silly old basket!

Citizen. What did you say?

Cicely. I was asking my assistant to get another bale from the basket, sir. Now this, sir, at four groats——

Citizen. Too much, I tell you.

Cicely. Well, then, sir—there's this at only two and a half groats.

Citizen. That is more my figure.

Cicely. Measure the gentleman, Simon.

(Simon *produces a vast tape-measure and makes a great fuss of taking the measurements—shoulder to elbow, elbow to wrist, back, shoulders, waist*)

Simon. Six.

Cicely (*writing it down in a huge book*) Six.

Simon. Nine.

Cicely. Nine.

Simon. Eight.
Cicely. Eight.
Simon (*at waist*) Sixty.
Cicely. Impossible!
Simon. It is.
Cicely. Pull!
Simon. That's better—fifty-eight.
Cicely. Pull again! Let me try.

(Cicely *comes out to help, each pulling one end of the measure*)

Now then! Fifty-seven—fifty-six—fifty-four——
Citizen. Ow! Will you leave my waist line alone, Madam!
Cicely. I'm sorry, sir; I quite forgot you were in it. Waist-line fifty-four. Well, that's settled.
Citizen. Oh, I don't know about that.
Cicely. What do you mean, "you don't know"?
Citizen. Is it strong? Is it good value? Will it wear well?
Cicely. We are not in the habit, sir, of selling shoddy articles at this establishment.
Citizen. The cloth I bought here ten years ago has not worn well. It has got quite thin. And the colour has faded.
Cicely. Do you mean to tell me, sir, that you have the impudence to stand there and tell me you're dissatisfied with the goods sold at this emporium?
Citizen. I beg your pardon, Madam?
Cicely. So you ought to do, you mean old crow.
Citizen. Really!
Cicely. You come in here with your mumblings and your East wind and your two and a half groats and have the sauce to tell me you aren't satisfied! You'll take what you're offered—see?
Citizen. Never in all my life——
Cicely (*seizing the tailor's shears*) And if I have any more non-sense from you I'll cut your beard off. You asked for some cloth and cloth you shall have and what's more you shall take it home with you on our special delivery service—come on, Simon!

(*Together they run round and round him with a bale of material and wrap him up like a parcel*)

Now then, out you go.

(*The Citizen is shot out of the door*)

The impudence! Anybody'd think——
Dick. Well, Dame Suett, I don't see where the customer is always right comes in.
Cicely. Oh, he was right enough, Dick. The cloth won't wear and the colour runs. What d'you expect at that price? Now out of my way, there's a good lad; it's time I was making the rhubarb

tart. Take off your coat, and look business-like and see what you can do. Now then, Simon, I want you.

SIMON. Yes, Dame Suett.

(*Exeunt* SIMON *and* CICELY SUETT. DICK *takes his coat off, humming a tune, and hangs it up near the counter. With his back to the door he does not see* ALICE *come in. She is halfway across the scene when he turns*)

DICK (*turning*) Miss Alice!

ALICE. Good morning, Master Whittington. For a moment I thought there was no-one here. I have been hurrying. There was someone in the street I did not want to meet. I——

(*Enter* MARMADUKE BUNG)

MARMADUKE. Ah! Mistress Alice—I have caught up with you.

ALICE. Good day, sir.

MARMADUKE. I saw you in the street and I was afraid I had lost you. But I am a persevering man, Mistress Alice, and I made all the speed that I could, consistent with an appearance of dignity, and I have succeeded in my quest. I have come, Mistress Alice, on purpose to invite you to a morning's pleasure.

ALICE. Indeed, sir?

MARMADUKE. Yes, Mistress Alice, a morning's pleasure. You are to walk with me in my father's garden, an' it please you—as I am sure it must.

ALICE. I am much obliged to you, Master Bung, for your consideration, but . . . I fear . . . I fear that that is impossible.

MARMADUKE. Impossible!

ALICE. Yes, sir—I regret to say that I am obliged to be within doors this morning. I have undertaken to—er—to dress the asparagus for my father's dinner.

MARMADUKE. That will not take long, Mistress Alice.

ALICE. Indeed it will, sir. I have to cut it, and wash it, and tie it in little bundles, and—and—put it in boiling water: it will take a long time.

MARMADUKE. I am sorry that duty should deny you the pleasure of my company today: but you must not neglect the service of your father. We men must be served and that is my comfort. One day, Mistress Alice, you shall dress asparagus for me. Eh? H'm! I wonder Master Fitzwarren should leave his safe door open like this. Is it wise?

ALICE. I expect my father knows what he is about, sir.

MARMADUKE. I hope he does, Mistress Alice. But there are thieves and cut-purses about. (*He looks at Dick*) We cannot be too careful.

ALICE. Good day, sir.

MARMADUKE. Good day, Mistress Alice.

(*Exit* MARMADUKE)

Alice. Oh, Dick!

Dick. Miss Alice!

Alice. What shall I do? I am supposed to marry that creature. I cannot, cannot do it.

Dick. If you cannot, Miss Alice, you may be sure you will not.

Alice. Do you think so?

Dick. I'm sure of it.

Alice. If I could only believe it!

Dick. Don't you love anyone else, Miss Alice?

Alice. Yes, Dick, I think I do.

Dick. Can't he help you, Miss?

Alice. I don't know if *he* loves *me*, Dick.

Dick. You don't *know*! But of course he does. He loves you like —like——

Alice. Like what, Dick? And how do you know?

Dick. He told me, Miss. He said you were as sweet as a wild rose.

8. "If You Should Meet My Own True Love"

(Dick and Alice)

I

Dick.

> If you should meet my own true love
>> (Your lover said to me)
> O, tell her she is sweet, oh sweet,
>> As a wild rose tree.
> The rose's leaf is like a heart.
>> And would that hers was free—
> O, if you should meet my own true love,
>> Ask her to wait for me.

II

Alice.

> If you should meet my love again,
>> Give him this answer true:
> The wild rose waits till a summer's day,
>> And I wait too.
> As long as roses deck the hedge
>> Beside the greenwood tree,
> So long I'll wait for my own true love
>> If he will wait for me.

Both.

> So long I'll wait for my true love
>> If $\left\{\begin{matrix} \text{she} \\ \text{he} \end{matrix}\right\}$ will wait for me.

(For the first time they sink into each other's arms)

Scene 4

Scene—*A London Street.*

Enter Marmaduke Bung, r. *Standing motionless,* l, *is* King Rat, *cloaked and hatted like a London citizen, but visibly red-tighted underneath.*

Marmaduke. Oh! I'm so angry! I ask Mistress Alice to come for a walk in my father's garden and she says no, she's got to dress the asparagus for dinner—and then I look through the window and see her singing songs with another man—that Whittington! I knew he was a scoundrel. If he should distract her affection I shall do something desperate—I feel sure I shall.

    What can a man do when oppressive Fate
    Obtrudes betwixt him and his promised mate?
    Cast him beneath the waves of yonder stream?
    Or hang himself upon the garret beam?
    Or cut his throat, or starve himself to death?
    How shall he find a means to stop his breath?
    How shall he take—

King Rat (*who has edged up silently*)
               I pray you, pardon me,
    May I intrude on your soliloquy?
    Chancing this way, good sir, on business bent,
    I overheard your piteous lament.
    Alas! These horrid schemes against survival
    Will hurt *yourself*, and not your filthy rival.
    Were it not sweeter, sir, by methods base,
    To lure this stinkard to some vile disgrace?
Marmaduke.
    Indeed, sir, yes—but how achieve this end?
King Rat.
    Tush! You are far too simple, gentle friend!
    Smirch his good name! Befoul his reputation!
    Tangle his feet by crooked accusation!
    Master Fitzwarren, sir, in my belief
    Would not retain the service of . . . *a thief*.
Marmaduke.
    If I conceive you rightly, kindly stranger,
    This conversation's not devoid of danger.
    Should we be overheard—
King Rat.   Precisely. Come,
    Let us withdraw awhile to yonder slum.
    There will I teach thee in my dismal cot
    The dirty details of a dastard plot.
Marmaduke.
    Pray, sir, lead on.

King Rat (*with an obsequious bow*)
> I follow, Master Bung.

(*Exit* Marmaduke, l)

Haha! But hush! King Rat must hold his tongue.

(*Exit* King Rat)

Scene 5

Scene—*Alderman Fitzwarren's shop.*

When the Curtain *rises* Dick *is at the counter putting things away. He sings a reprise chorus of "Put your best foot forward". He plays ball with the* Cat. *Enter* Marmaduke Bung.

Marmaduke. H'm. You keep shop in a strange way, Master Whittington.

Dick. Well, there weren't any customers, Master Bung.

Marmaduke. It is not what Alderman Fitzwarren is accustomed to.

Dick. Maybe not, but I don't know what business it is of yours, sir. What can I do for you? I suppose you do want something?

Marmaduke. I will be much obliged if you will tell Miss Alice I would be glad to speak to her.

Dick. What—again?

Marmaduke. Yes, sir—will you kindly take that message?

Dick. Oh . . . Very well.

Marmaduke. Thank you, sir.

(*Exit* Dick)

Hohoho! Now—softly!

(*Melodrama chords as* Marmaduke *goes to the open safe*)

Just as I hoped! Haha!

(Marmaduke *removes money bags and puts them in the pockets of Dick's coat, which is hanging on a peg. The* Cat *sees all this and attempts sundry scratches and buffets*)

Now, Master Dick—we shall see what comes of your fine aspirations. Hahaha—ha!

(*Enter* Alderman Fitzwarren)

Fitzwarren. Bless my soul, Master Bung! All alone? The shop unattended? Whittington should be on duty. Where is the boy?

MARMADUKE. I thought it strange, sir. There was no-one here when I came in five minutes ago.

FITZWARREN. No-one?

MARMADUKE. And I thought it wise, sir, to keep guard.

FITZWARREN. That was very kind of you, Master Bung.

MARMADUKE. Especially, sir, as I could not help noticing that your safe was open. I trust——

FITZWARREN. It is all right, Master Bung, I opened it myself. And at the very moment I was called away to receive the Lord Mayor. I have been so immersed in business, Master Bung, that I had quite forgotten it. How careless of me!

MARMADUKE. I must agree, sir, that it was unwise. I trust everything is as it should be, sir.

FITZWARREN. I hardly think—Oh!

MARMADUKE. Is anything the matter, sir?

FITZWARREN. The matter, Master Bung! It is gone! My week's takings vanished!

MARMADUKE. And that Whittington vanished, too.

FITZWARREN. Surely, Master Bung, you don't think . . .? Dame Cicely! Alice! Simon! Sally! Whittington! Come hither at once!

(*Enter* ALDERMAN BUNG *from the street*)

BUNG. What is the matter, my good sir?

FITZWARREN. I have been robbed, sir.

BUNG. Robbed? Great heavens!

(*Enter* ALICE, CICELY SUETT, SIMON, SALLY *from the house*)

ALICE. What is the matter, dear father?

FITZWARREN. I have been robbed.

ALL. Robbed?

FITZWARREN. Where is that Whittington?

(*Enter* DICK)

DICK. Here I am, sir. What is amiss?

FITZWARREN. Oh, you're there, are you? Why were you not on duty in the shop?

DICK. I was, sir—until Master Bung asked me to fetch Miss Alice hither.

FITZWARREN. Simon—run at once to the watch——

MARMADUKE. Should we not first make sure, sir, that the money is not still on the premises.

BUNG. Yes, Master Fitzwarren, my son is right. Each person should be searched.

CICELY. Searched!

FITZWARREN. I cannot doubt my own household, sir.

Bung. You are too trusting, my friend.

Dick. Nay, Master Fitzwarren—Master Bung is quite right. I have no objection.

Marmaduke. Let me see, sir. No—nothing there.

Alice. Thank heaven!

Marmaduke. But your coat, sir. Where is your coat?

Dick. There.

Marmaduke. A strange place to leave it, sir. Perhaps it was handy for your departure, sir.

Dick. What do you mean, sir?

Marmaduke. I mean, sir, that your villainy has not succeeded. You are exposed, sir. Look, Alderman Fitzwarren!

All. Ooh!

Marmaduke. Are these your money bags?

All. Ooh!

Fitzwarren. I cannot believe this.

Dick. Sir—*do* not believe it! I never stole your money.

Cicely. Of course he didn't.

Dick. Someone has put the money in my pocket to disgrace me.

Cicely. Of course they have.

Dick. You must believe me, sir.

Alice. Father, you must believe him.

Fitzwarren. Alice, my child, I would not wish to accuse an innocent man.

Cicely. That's just what you're doing.

Fitzwarren. Be silent, Cicely.

Cicely. I will not.

Fitzwarren. But we cannot dismiss the evidence of our eyes.

Marmaduke. And what do you know of this man, Mistress Alice?

Bung. Did I not warn you, sir?

Fitzwarren. You did, Master Bung, and I fear you are all too justified. Whittington, I had a mind to like you, and I am grieved to find my trust misplaced. Since I have lost nothing I will not prosecute you. But you must leave my house at once.

Cicely. It's a shame.

Dick. What do you say, Mistress Alice?

Alice. I cannot believe you did this thing.

Dick. Your daughter accepts my word, sir. But if you will not —I will go and gladly.

Fitzwarren. Go, sir! And never darken these doors again.

Bung. Be off with you!

Marmaduke. Get out!

Dick. Good-bye, Mistress Alice. Will you wait for me till my name has been cleared?

Alice. Trust me, Dick——

Dick and Alice (*singing*)
> So long as roses deck the hedge
> Beside the greenwood tree,
> So long I'll wait for my true love
> If {he / she} will wait for me.

(*The* Cat *springs at* Marmaduke. *He screams*)

Dick. Come, Puss.

(*Exeunt* Dick *and the* Cat)

Fitzwarren. This has been a great shock to me, a great shock. But it is a lesson, Alice, a lesson. I cannot let you return to your various tasks until I have pointed out the serious consequences of this kind of behaviour. Come—gather round—and let me tell you the story of my own early life.

All. Oh, *no*, Alderman Fitzwarren.

Simon. You told us about that last week, sir.

Fitzwarren. I cannot let an occasion like this pass without pointing out something or other. I shall certainly tell you about the poor man who found a purse and was rewarded for his honesty. And I shall be much obliged if you will pay attention and join in at the appropriate places.

9. "It Always Pays Best to be Honest"

(Fitzwarren, Alice and Chorus)

I

Fitzwarren.
> A poor man was walking in London
> His innocent daughter beside,
> When there on the pavement before him
> A large bag of money he spied.
> He was placing the purse in his pocket
> Intending to spend it on bread,
> When sudden a gentle hand stopped him
> And softly the little one said—

Alice.
> "It always pays best to be honest;
> It's a policy all can afford;
> For you may go to prison for stealing
> But honesty brings a reward."

II

Fitzwarren.
> So touched was the man by this warning
> That he took his small daughter's advice,

Brought most of the gold to its owner,
  And received a reward in a trice,
And the child grasped the hand of her parent,

ALICE.
  And cried, "I shall sing this refrain
To urge the same conduct, dear Father,
  Whenever this happens again—

ALL.
    It always pays best to be honest;
      It's a policy all can afford;
    For you may go to prison for stealing
      But honesty brings a reward."

III

FITZWARREN.
  That poor man became so successful
    And gathered so splendid a hoard,
That he soon was a freeman of London
    And married his child to a lord—
And when asked how he built up his business,
    Contriving such riches to gain,
He looks at his innocent daughter
    And answers the world in this strain—

ALL.
    "It always pays best to be honest;
      It's a policy all can afford;
    For you may go to prison for stealing
      But honesty brings a reward."

SCENE 6

SCENE—*A London Street.*

Enter, L, KING RAT, *in an ecstasy of pleasure.*

KING RAT.
  Haha! haha! Haha! Hoho! Hehe!
  There was a triumph of chicanery!
  A pest upon it! I have been too proud,
  Forgot my lesson and have laughed too loud.
  Look where she comes on hateful virtuous wing!

(*Enter* SNOWFLAKE)

SNOWFLAKE.
  What dost thou here, corrupt and evil thing,
  Spoiling our charming Christmas celebration
  With these disgusting peals of cachination?

KING RAT.
What do I here? What reason makes me gay?
Much mischief have I wrought this happy day.
Too late you come to strive against King Rat!
Dick Whittington and his detested cat
Are even now cast forth with none to trust in,
Their home the gutter and their food the dustbin.
SNOWFLAKE.
Vile creature! Dost thou dare with arts obscene
In London's happy streets to intervene?
Know then, thou treacherous and abandoned swine,
I have a potent spell worth two of thine.
Thou canst not scare me with thy vulgar roar—
Love is the key that opens every door.
(*She waves her wand*)
KING RAT.
Ten thousand devils that my plan should fail
And bring this busybody on my trail,
Who dares to speak in Love's accursed name,
Searing my vitals like a furnace flame.
I'll foil you yet! In yonder blasted oak
I have the details of a counter stroke—
Think not you've heard the last of my foul laughter!
Fare ill for now! We meet again hereafter!

(*Exit* KING RAT)

SNOWFLAKE.
Really! The people that one has to meet
To keep our panto reasonably sweet!
Yet what care I for insult or applause
If I can aid Love's all-demanding cause?
Love is a power most strange and most profound.
It conquers all; it turns the world around;
No obstacle its mission can delay,
For, come what shall, Love will find out the way.
Nay, more than this, it has a curious skill
To transubstantiate itself at will,
And so become, by some mysterious law,
A key with art to open every door.

(SNOWFLAKE *beckons to her right and a flight of* FAIRIES *hastens in
and forms a group around her during the introductory music of the song*)

10. "MY BOSOM IS A BOWER" (SNOWFLAKE and CHORUS)

I

SNOWFLAKE.

My bosom is a bower
Up many a winding stair,

And only he who pleases me
  Shall find a welcome there.
A prisoner, I do not grieve,
  Or murmur at my fate—
Love is the key, the sesame,
  Shall ope the castle gate.
Love is the key, the sesame,
  Shall ope the castle gate.

CHORUS.

Shall ope the castle gate,

SNOWFLAKE.

Ah me!

CHORUS.

Shall ope the castle gate—

SNOWFLAKE.

Ah me!

SNOWFLAKE *and* CHORUS.

Love is the key, the sesame,
Shall ope the castle gate.

II

SNOWFLAKE.

The key that guards my bower
  Is not of metal made,
And only he who pleases me
  Shall profit from its aid.
Intangible to vulgar hands,
  I cherish it the more—
Love is the key, the sesame,
  That opes my bosom's door.
Love is the key, the sesame,
  That opes my bosom's door.

CHORUS.

That opes my bosom's door,

SNOWFLAKE.

Ah me!

CHORUS.

That opes my bosom's door
Love is the key, the sesame,
That opes my bosom's door.

SNOWFLAKE.

Heigho for love, my dears!

CHORUS   Heigho!

SNOWFLAKE.   Heigho!

But come! We stay too long! 'Tis time to go.
Twilight draws on, and all must very soon
Be dancing gaily 'neath the mad May moon.

Tonight, my dears, it is my fairy will
You hold your revels upon yonder hill,
For there, if I have read the signs aright,
Our hero, Dick, will pass this very night.
Delay him till I come in gentle slumber
By dancing round him some romantic number,
Sylphides, Giselle, or something on a par,
Selected from your elfin repertoire.
Away! I'll join you on the hill-top green
When I've devised our transformation scene.

(*Exeunt* FAIRIES)

That's my dear girls! And now, O Power of Love,
Exert thy potent influence above!
Direct my plans, and fill with eager hopes
Those honest hearts who operate the ropes,
Dispose thy Ministers to use each switch
With due discretion, pondering which is which,
And thus, in one inspired co-ordination,
Produce a really splendid transformation!
Come, hands unseen, exert your utmost skill,
And swift transport our scene to Highgate Hill.

(*Powder-flash. Exit* SNOWFLAKE)

SCENE 7

SCENE—*Highgate Hill. A half-stage picture.*

Enter DICK *and the* CAT.

DICK. Well, Puss, here we are, on the tramp again—one day on the top, the next on the bottom. I used to hear voices in the bells of London, leading me on to success. Now they're just bells —ding-dong, ding-dong. What do you make of it, Puss? Are we done for?

11. BALLET AND FINALE ACT I

CAT. Miaiou!
DICK. Shall we fight back and make our fortunes?
CAT. Miaiou!
DICK. You think so, do you? Well, that's something. All right, Puss. Tomorrow—tomorrow we'll see what we can do about it— but now—let's sleep—sleep—sleep. Hey! I'm weary.

(DICK *lies down.*
Ballet, including a dance for the Cat and a White Cat, and other characters in the pantomime if desired. At the end enter SNOWFLAKE)

SNOWFLAKE.
Awake, Dick Whittington.

DICK.   Who calls?
SNOWFLAKE.   'Tis I,
  The guardian spirit of your destiny.
  I know your troubles, Dick. Be not downcast!
  My magic art perceives they will not last.
  Evil, like grit in some involved machine,
  May sometimes triumph like a thing unclean—
  But never doubt! Long 'ere the engine spoil
  Comes Love, the foreman, with his can of oil.
  All shall conspire for good, if you'll agree
  To place your trust implicitly in me.
DICK.
  I'll follow your commands, I promise you.
SNOWFLAKE.
  Then hearken to the thing that you must do.
  The stars, the tea-leaves, and my magic crystal,
  All indicate that you must go to Bristol,
  That lovely city with its famous haven
  Embowered upon the flowery banks of Avon.
  From there take ship 'neath an auspicious star
  And journey to the coast of Africa,
  Where, I perceive, in spite of sundry hitches
  You will amass a vast amount of riches.
  And, better far, dear boy, as you must see,
  Strike a shrewd blow for moral probity.

(*Music*)

SNOWFLAKE.
  Hark to the bells of London, how they ring!
  Can you not hear the promises they sing?
VOICES.
  Turn again, Whittington!
    Thou worthy citizen
  Lord Mayor of London.
DICK.
  Lord Mayor of London! Why, 'tis impossible.
SNOWFLAKE.
  Wonder not, Dick, at what the steeples tell!
  Take my advice and all shall yet be well.
  Fear not for aught the future holds in store—
  Love is the key that opens every door.
DICK.
  Fairy, I am in love, and I'll obey
  All that Love bids me, this and every day.
SNOWFLAKE.
  Dear boy! No further words! Delay no longer!
  Lo! In the orient sky the light grows stronger—

And see! My magic art, by Love bestowed,
Enables me to set you on your road.
The morning mists dissolve—your task's begun—
Yonder lies Bristol in the rising sun!

(11. *Music. The Highgate Hill drop dissolves (if it be a gauze) or rises, and reveals a hedge-row with a stile and, beyond it, rising ground and a distant prospect of Bristol.* DICK *turns with wonder and walks towards the stile*)

VOICES.
   Turn again, Whittington! Thou worthy citizen!
   Lord Mayor of London.
SNOWFLAKE.
   Return with honour, Dick!
DICK (*singing*)
            If you should meet my own true love
               Give her this word from me—
            Tell her my love is just as strong
               As a wild rose tree.

FAIRIES.
            As long as roses deck the hedge
               Beside the greenwood tree
SOLO CHORISTER.
            So long you'll wait for your true love,
               If she will wait for you—

(*During the chorus* DICK *mounts the stile. He turns to wave from the rising ground on the other side as the curtain falls*)

ACT II

Scene i

Scene—*The Bristol Docks.*
 At the back of the scene, "The Saucy Alice" is tied up alongside the quay, with a gang-plank leading from ship to shore. R *is a big barrel and a bench,* L *several more barrels.*

When the Curtain *rises the* Crew *of the "The Saucy Alice" are indulging in a heaty chorus on the quay.*

12. "Hornpipe" (Sailors)

I

Sailors.
  With a hi-yo-ha!
  And good-bye to pa and ma—
  With a hi-yo-ha!
  For we're off to Africa—
  Seeking gold and apes and ivory,
  And incidental wivery,
  For everybody knows what English sailors are,
  For everybody knows what English sailors are,
  And everybody knows what English sailors are,
  Seeking gold and apes and ivory,
  And incidental wivery,
  Among the sunny scenery of Africa.

II

  With a hi-yo-ha!
  And good-bye to pa and ma—
  With a hi-yo-ha!
  We are travelling afar—
  And you know how far a Tar goes
  When he's after precious cargoes
  And the beauties of the scenery in Africa,
  And the beauties of the scenery in Africa,
  And the beauties of the scenery in Africa—
  And you know how far a Tar goes
  When he's after precious cargoes
  And the beauties of the scenery in Africa.

(*The music quickens, and the* CREW *give an energetic performance of the Sailors' Hornpipe, returning to the words to bring the whole thing to a finish. The* MATE, *who has been watching from the deck of "The Saucy Alice", comes down the gang-plank*)

MATE. Now then, men—a hornpipe's a very nice thing in its proper place, and I'm proud to see you have paid so much attention to your dancing—but you must set to work, lads.

SAILORS. Work!

MATE. Aye, my hearties.

IST SAILOR. Things have come to a pretty pass, your honour, when honest sailoring men be asked to work.

SAILORS. Aye—that they has.

MATE. I know how you feel, lads, but the *Alice* is due to sail on the next tide, and it's time you was a'loading of the cargo.

IST SAILOR. We're short-handed, your honour.

SAILORS. Aye, that we be.

COOK (*a little man*) And I'll tell you something else, Mr Mate.

MATE. What's that, Cook?

COOK. I'm not sailing in your ship anyway. I'm not going to cook any longer in that rotten rat-ridden old galley of yours, and that's flat, and I wish you a very good arternoon.

(*Exit* COOK)

MATE. But, Cook!—Men, I appeal to you——

(*The* CREW *gather round the Mate. Enter* DICK *and* PUSS. *They stand, listening, on the edge of the crowd*)

IST SAILOR. Get us the crew, Mr Mate, and we'll do our duty —but we're a man short.

2ND SAILOR. And we ain't going to sea without a cook.

SAILORS. Aye. That we ain't.

MATE. Shiver my quarterdeck! Will you listen to me? Think of the money you're all going to earn on this trip. All that gold and ivory—all them apes.

IST SAILOR. We shan't never get to Africa without a proper crew.

SAILORS. Nay. That we shan't.

DICK. Mr Mate!

MATE. Aye—who's that?

DICK. If it's a man you want, sir——

MATE. What's that?

DICK. My name's Dick Whittington, sir, and, if you're a man short, will you take me? I want a ship——

(*The* SAILORS *laugh*)

MATE. Oh, you want a ship, do you?

DICK. And this is my cat, Puss, the best rat-catcher in the world.

Puss. Wow!
Mate. Well, that's something, and you want to go to sea?
Dick. Yes, sir.
Mate. Ever been to sea before?
Dick. No, sir.
Mate. Ever done any hard work in your life?
Dick. Oh, yes, sir——
Mate. What was your last job?
Dick. I was a draper's apprentice, sir.

(*The* Sailors *laugh*)

Mate. And ran away, I suppose.
Dick. Well——
1st Sailor. See here, your honour, we want a sailor aboard of *The Saucy Alice*—not some lily-fingered baby who's spent his life measuring whimples for ladies.
2nd Sailor. What good's a boy like this? I could chuck him over my shoulder with one hand.
Dick. You try it.
2nd Sailor. What did you say, you shrimp?
Dick. I said you try it.
2nd Sailor. Cor splice my bulwarks!
3rd Sailor. Go on, Jack. Hit him in the scuppers.
2nd Sailor. Come 'ere, you miserable bit of ground-bait. Now then—what shall I do with you, eh?
3rd Sailor. Pitch him in the harbour.
Dick. Let go—or you'll suffer for it.

(*Laughter*)

2nd Sailor. Split my braces!—what was that?
Dick. I told you to let go

(*Laughter*)

but—if you want a fight—look out!

(Dick *pushes himself away, and squares up to the Sailor. Amid cries of encouragement and surprise a fight begins, in which the nimbleness of* Dick *is altogether too much for the lumbering* 2nd Sailor, *who does everything possible wrong, and is finally knocked out flat. The* Cat *sits on top of him*)

Mate. Well, that settles that, men. If Dick Whittington is good enough for Filthy Jack Hopkins, he's good enough to serve in *The Saucy Alice*.
Sailors. Aye. He'll do. You're welcome, messmate.
Mate. Very good. Then will you get on with the loading, you lubbers.
3rd Sailor. What about the cook?
Sailors. Aye. We ain't going to sea without no cook.

Mate. Split my mainsail! Will you do your work and leave that to me? Get on with you!

(*The* Sailors, *with some grumbling, go off on the* l, *presumed position of the cargo, carrying* Filthy Jack Hopkins)

Now then—any experience?

Dick. None, sir.

Mate. That will be helpful, I'm sure. Still—can't be helped. Come on—and stow your gear on board—and bring your Cat. We can do with him in the *Alice*, I can tell you.

Dick. Right, sir. Go on, Puss.

(*The* Mate *goes up the gang-plank, followed by* Puss. *But, as* Dick *is about to follow,* Cicely *peeps out from a place of concealment on the* r, *and pokes him with her umbrella*)

Cicely. Dick!

Dick. Cicely!

Mate. Come on, there.

Dick. One moment, sir—I've just got to get my bundle.

(*The* Mate *disappears*)

Cicely. Bundle indeed!

Dick. Didn't mean you, dear. How did you get here?

Cicely. Had a row with Alderman Fitzwarren, my dear. Turned from the house. Cast out. So I decided to follow you. Never thought I'd be in time—but I met a funny old lady who helped me on my way. She knew you, she said, and asked me to give you a message. Don't forget, she says, that Love is the key that opens every door.

Dick. It was my fairy! That means everything's going to be all right; I'm sure of it. I've just joined the crew of *The Saucy Alice* —chose her because of the name—and we're sailing on the next tide.

Cicely. Good! I'm coming too.

Dick. What?

Cicely. Certainly. Of course I am. You've got to get me on board somehow.

Mate (*from somewhere on board the "Alice"*) Here you, where the devil are you?

Dick. Hide, Cicely!

Cicely. What's the good of hiding?

Dick. You must—till we've thought of something. Inside this barrel.

(Cicely *climbs into the big barrel on the* r)

Mate (*reappearing*) Burst my buttons! Where are you?

Dick. Here, sir.

Cicely. Do what you can!

Dick. Keep down!

Mate. Why don't you come aboard?

Cicely (*popping up*) And get me something to drink! I'm dry as old bones.

Dick. Sorry, sir. Couldn't find my bundle, sir.

Mate (*coming down gang-plank with a can of ale*) Well, get on board with it quick, and then come back to me.

Dick. Aye aye, sir.

(Dick *goes on board. The* Mate *sits down on the bench and is about to drink when he sees something off* l)

Mate. Curry my capstan! What are them swabs up to now? (*He puts down his can on the bench and crosses the quay*) Hi—you there!

(Cicely *pops up and takes the can. A* Sailor *enters in answer to the* Mate's *call*)

What in the name of Neptune do you think you're a'doing of with them blasted barrels?

4th Sailor. We was putting the blazing things on the perishing deck, your honour, with the rest of the flaming cargo.

Mate. Well, you can fizzing well take 'em off again. What do you think I've just brought 'em 'ere for all the way from Portugal, you saturated sissy.

4th Sailor. I'm sure I'm sorry, Mr Mate. I'll rectify that foolish mistake in one half of a ruddy moment.

(*Exit* Sailor. *The* Mate *turns towards the bench, and* Dick *comes down the gang-plank*)

Mate. Cor pickle my port-hole . . . Hey! Where's my drink? (*Turning to Dick, so that his back is to the barrel*) Have you been pinching my liquor, you? For if you have, boy . . .

Dick. I haven't touched it, sir.

Mate. I put my ale down on that there bench not two minutes ago and the moment I turns me back some lubber . . .

(Cicely *pops up and puts the can back*)

Dick. Are you sure, sir?

Mate. I tell you it was there—there on the—well, that's the most extraordinary thing—I could have sworn . . . All right— (*turns back to Dick*) go on and help with that last lot of cargo. And then there's these barrels (*indicates those on the* l) to be put aboard last of all.

(Cicely *has popped up and taken the can again*)

Dick. Aye, aye, sir.

(*Exit* Dick)

Mate. Eh? what's this—*what's* this? Am I going off my rocker?

(*The* MATE *puts his hands over his eyes and turns away.* CICELY *pops up. He turns back.* CICELY *pops down. He turns away again.* CICELY *pops up. He turns back. She pops down. He turns away. She pops up and puts the can back. He turns back*)

Rattle my rudder! It must be liver. Another can of ale'll put that right. (*He grabs the drink, then calls to the Sailors off*) Hey—you! And you! Up with these flipping barrels.

(*Enter* 3RD SAILOR)

3RD SAILOR. All of 'em, sir?
MATE. No—only them barrels on this side. Not those on t'other.

(*A scene of activity follows, during which, with much shouting of directions,* SAILORS *take the three barrels on the* L *to the gang-plank.* CICELY, *realizing that she's on the wrong side, endeavours to move herself across, by little runs and shuffles.* DICK *tries to help by bustling round the barrel from time to time to cover things up*)

Not that barrel. Didn't you hear what I said?
DICK. Aye, aye, sir.
1ST SAILOR. Roll 'em up! Up you go! One. Two. Three. What about this one here, sir?

(CICELY *is stuck in the middle of the stage*)

MATE. Eh? Half a minute . . . Half a minute. That there barrel weren't there a moment ago, I'll swear. What's going on?

(*Everyone pauses to look. Dead silence.* CICELY *innocently does another shuffle. Before the fascinated gaze of the whole crew, she peeps out— shuffles a little further and then cautiously sticks up her umbrella handle by way of a periscope. The* MATE *sends two* SAILORS *across. They tip up the barrel and out rolls* CICELY)

Now then—what's all this?
1ST SAILOR. Stowaway, sir.
MATE. Stowaway. Take a bit of stowing to put that away. What are you doing here, you old bag?
CICELY. I want to go to Africa.
MATE. Well, you won't go on my ship. Take her particulars.
1ST SAILOR. Name?
CICELY. Cicely Suett.
1ST SAILOR. Age?
CICELY. Shan't tell you.
1ST SAILOR. Profession?
CICELY. Cook.
MATE. What's that? Cook, did you say?
CICELY. Aye, aye, sir.

Dick. Excuse me, sir, but I know Dame Suett. She's honest, sir, and a wonderful cook. If you——

Mate. Why, burst my bowsprit! I've got it! You *shall* sail, you old bundle. You shall be ship's cook.

2nd Sailor. A woman aboard! That's unlucky, Mr Mate.

Sailors. Aye.

Mate. Souse my mainmast! I say I'll have her.

3rd Sailor. But can the old faggot cook, your honour?

2nd Sailor. Yes, Mr Mate! We got to know that.

Sailors. Aye! That we do.

1st Sailor. And do she understand the ways of sailoring men?

Cicely. Do I understand the ways of sailoring men, you old crab-pot? I should think I do. Split my fathingale, Mr Mate, if you want any help from me it'll be on my terms, see?

13. "Rattle My Binnacle" (Cicely)

I

Cicely.

Rattle my binnacle!
Sailors are cynical
Girls of my figure have got to beware,
The trouble with chaps is
They're subject to lapses—
The trouble with sailors is sailors don't care.
So don't come and dally
Around in my galley—
You won't get your dinner unless you behave.
If you start getting tough
You'll have nothing but duff—
Sing hey for a life on the billowy wave!
Sing hey for a life on the ocean,
Sing ho for a life at sea!
Sing hey for a life of devotion!
Sing ho for a life on the sea!

II

Mariners cherish
A curious relish
For saying a Briton's a right to be free—
But rattle my compass!
I'll kick up a rumpus
If anyone tries any freedom with me.
So stick to your fishes,
And leave me the dishes—
You won't get your dinner unless you behave.
If you try any sauce
You'll get nothing but horse—

Sing hey for a life on the billowy wave!
Sing hey for a life on the ocean,
Sing ho for a life at sea!
Sing hey for a life of devotion!
Sing ho for a life on the sea!

III

Oh! Rattle my kettle!
When I'm on my mettle,
There isn't a cook in the world to compare.
But it isn't all gravy
To work for the navy—
The trouble with sailors is sailors don't care.
I'll banish such evils
As scurvy and weevils,
Provided you sailors will try to behave—
And if you're all good
There'll be plenty of pud—
Sing hey for a life on the billowy wave!
Sing hey for a life on the ocean,
Sing ho for a life at sea!
Sing hey for a life of devotion!
Sing ho for a life on the sea!

Shiver my saucepan! Them's my terms, Mr Mate—do you accept of them?

MATE. Very gladly, Dame Suett. I like your spirit, and I'll be glad to have you in the crew. Do you agree, men?

SAILORS. Aye!

MATE. Then, burst my cistern! We can leave on the next tide. The wind's right. Cargo's aboard. Everything ready?

1ST SAILOR. Aye, aye, sir. All shipshape and Bristol fashion.

MATE. Very good. All aboard then!

14. "SHIPSHAPE AND BRISTOL FASHION"

(MATE, DICK, CICELY and SAILORS)

I

DICK.

Shipshape and Bristol fashion—
That's the way to be going to sea.

CICELY.

On any other terms of locomotion
I wouldn't trust myself upon the ocean—

MATE.

We've got plenty able seamen

Cicely.
          And the Mate's a perfect demon,
Dick.
          So we'll bound across the briny like a bee—
Dick, Mate *and* Cicely.
          O! Shipshape and Bristol fashion
          That's the shape and the fashion for me.
All.
          Ods bobs!
          The shape and the fashion for me.

II

All.
          Shipshape and Bristol fashion—
               That's the way to be going to sea.
          On any other terms of locomotion
               I wouldn't trust myself upon the ocean—
Dick, Mate *and* Cicely.
          But where mariners are able
          We can bravely slip the cable
          And we'll bound across the briny like a bee—
          O! Shipshape and Bristol fashion
All.
          That's the shape and the fashion for me.
               Ods bobs!
          The shape and the fashion for me.

Mate. All aboard!
All. Hurrah!

(*Everyone rushes to the ship as the* Curtain *falls*)

SCENE 2

Scene—*A London Street.*

Enter Alice *with shopping bag. She crosses to the* L, *stops—turns about and hastens back the other way. She has seen* Marmaduke.

Marmaduke (*entering*) Mistress Alice! Oo-ooo!
     Did you not see me, Mistress Alice, waiting
     At my accustomed spot by yonder grating?
Alice. Really, Master Bung—I wish you would not speak to me in rhymed couplets.
Marmaduke. It's a habit I've got into lately, Mistress Alice.
Alice. It's a very disagreeable one.

D

MARMADUKE. Disagreeable, Mistress Alice? I hope you will see nothing disagreeable in me, who am determined to do everything in my power to make our lives an example of connubial pleasure.

ALICE. Master Bung, please do not use such unseemly phrases.

MARMADUKE. I only . . .

ALICE. Please do not follow me about . . .

MARMADUKE. But, Mistress Al . . .

ALICE. And please do not expect anything from me. I will not, will not marry you—and now you know.

(*Exit* ALICE)

MARMADUKE. Ooh!

(*Enter* KING RAT)

KING RAT.
  Hey! Master Bung!

MARMADUKE.   Dear sir!

KING RAT.   How now? What news?
  How did it prosper, eh? Our little ruse?

MARMADUKE. It worked precisely, sir, as you prophesied. Whittington is cast out.

KING RAT. Ha!

MARMADUKE. He went straight away, and no-one has heard of him since.

KING RAT.
  I knew that dog would come to a bad end—
  But why these troubled looks, my gentle friend?

MARMADUKE. Alas, sir, instead of conducing to my happiness, the whole affair has had a sad effect on my spirits. It is as though I had fallen into a moral decline, sir.

KING RAT. Ha!

MARMADUKE. I find myself increasingly impelled to make my entrances and exits on the left side, sir—the bad side of the street, if you'll excuse my saying so, sir. And I use a lot of bad words, like curse and blow, sir, and, I even find myself talking in rhymed couplets, like you do, sir. It is all very distressing. Besides, I am no nearer my ambition. Miss Alice rejects my advances—and while Whittington lives I fear she always will.

KING RAT.
  Precisely—while he lives . . .

MARMADUKE.   You don't suggest . . .

KING RAT.
  Nothing, dear sir, was further from this breast.
  Yet, should the Gods some tragedy contrive,
  It might be hard to keep the lad alive.
  Accidents happen, sir—

MARMADUKE.   My only fear is—

KING RAT.
   Good Master Bung, you raise too many queries
   Welcome the chance by kindly Fate afforded,
   However fishy, foul, or frankly sordid.
MARMADUKE.
   I will, dear sir.
KING RAT.   Good, good! I have a wheeze
   Shall bring this prig, this humbug, to his knees
   And will invite, to aid my foul design,
   A singularly nasty friend of mine.
   No words! I'll swift away, and in my den
   Write him a letter with my poisoned pen.

(*Exit* KING RAT)

MARMADUKE. What shall I do? He offers hope and comfort, and yet I know not whether to trust him. Can it be that I am being drawn imperceptibly into evil ways?
   Alas, what midnight horrors fill my brain!
   Surely my nerves will crack beneath the strain—
   Curse on these couplets! There I go again!

(*Exit* MARMADUKE, L. SALLY *and* SIMON *enter from the other side*)

SIMON. Well, I say, now that Dick and Cicely have gone, the story's bound to follow them—and if we don't get our song in now we never shall.
SALLY. All right, Simon. What shall it be? *Kitty in the Cowshed*— or *Hetty in the Hay*—that's nice—or what about *Maggie up the Maypole*?
SIMON. No, Sally—I'm sick of all them folk songs. I want to express my personality. To jazz it up—
SALLY. Jazz it up?
SIMON. That's the word, Sal. New sort of music I've invented. I shouldn't be surprised if they wasn't singing it hundreds of years hence—and no-one admitting, such, my girl, is the malignancy of a jealous Fate, that it was all invented in the fourteenth century by me, Simon Snatchpole.
SALLY. How does it go, Simon?
SIMON. Well—instead of te-tum-te-tum-te-tum——
SALLY. Yes.
SIMON. You've got to get a oomph into it.
SALLY. Oh?
SIMON. And a ho-ti-ho-to——
SALLY. Oh?
SIMON. And a hotch-cha-cha——
SALLY. You mean——
SIMON. Listen, my girl, I'll teach you. Here's my new number.
SALLY. Number?

Simon. Song, sweetie—and it's all about this little old town, London.

15. "Ra! Ra!" (Simon and Sally)

I

Simon.

Ra! Ra! There's no place on a par
  With this metropolis.
Alma mater's a first-rater—
  She's the top she is.
Guess I'm in communion
With this old commercial union
Of culture and plutocracy.
Oh Boy! I'm thorough
In my liking for this borough—
London is the burg for me.

Got it?
Sally. Think so——

II

Where, where is a place to compare
  With this community?

Simon.

No sir, no mum, dulce domum
  's good enough for me.

Sally.

Alderman and beadle,

Simon.

From Holborn to Threadneedle,

Sally.

They fill my heart with ecstasy.

Both.

And Boy! The power
Of that dear old Norman Tower!
London is the burg for me.

III

Simon.

Gee—whiz! There's no other like this
  Municipality.
Gog and Magog set me agog—
  They're the boys for me.

Both.

The Mayor and Corporation
Have my hearty approbation,

       I love each Guild and Company,
       O Boy! I'm thorough
       In my liking for that borough—
       London is the burg for me.

(*They dance and exeunt* SIMON *and* SALLY)

SCENE 3

SCENE—*The palace of Neptune, a superb scene of coral beauty.
An old chest, relic of some ancient wreck, stands in* C.

When the CURTAIN *rises enter* NEPTUNE *studying a scroll.*

NEPTUNE.
    Believe me, sir, I've heard this creature rave
    Against the deities of land and wave,
    And heap on Neptune his most vile aspersion,
    By rudely betting there was no such person.
    Eh?
    And with such sacrilegious words on lip,
    The bumptious braggart dares to board a ship—
    Which ship, by vulgar name, *The Saucy Alice*,
    Now sails the sea above your ocean palace.
    Be warned by me! In some pernicious hour
    The wretch may try the measure of your power.
    Strike, while you can, this stinkard and his cat.
    Ever your old infernal friend, King Rat.
    Winkles and Barnacles! Porpoise!

(*Enter* PORPOISE)

PORPOISE.
                           Here, dread Lord!
NEPTUNE.
    Haste to the surface—there keep watch and ward,
    Concealed among the ocean's crested white,
    Until a ship called *Alice* heaves in sight.
    The moment come, good Porpoise, cleave the waters,
    And bring the news, hot-fin, to my headquarters.
PORPOISE.
    I'll put a girdle round the earth—
NEPTUNE.   Enough!
    Cut out the poetry and do your stuff.

(*Exit* PORPOISE)

Beneath this crystal roof, beyond Man's thought
Deeper than anchor's fall I hold my court—
Since Time began the Tyrant of the Sea,
And shall this tadpole bandy cracks with me?

(Music *begins*)

Sing on, my seamaids, your eternal song!
The Saucy Alice shall be yours 'ere long.

(Neptune *strides off*. Sea Nymphs *arise from among the rocks and caves*)

16. "Lying on These Yellow Sands" (Sea Nymphs)

Sea Nymphs.

Lying on these yellow sands,
　　Beneath the towering sea,
Are lovely specimens
　　Of marine biology.
Shoals of shells and pearls and coral,
　　Fish that flash and flee,
And sleek and physically unique
　　There's me!
　　　　　Me!
　　　　　　Me!

Nimble little seamaids,
　　Diving through the waves,
Round we go, playing what d'ye know,
　　In the green sea caves.
Mermen join our revels
　　With light fantastic tread—
There's plenty of fun for a seamaid
　　On the ocean bed.
There's plenty of fun for a seamaid
　　On the ocean bed.
Swimming, diving,
　　Little hearts aglow
Singing songs the Sirens sang
　　A million years ago—
Davy Jones's treasures
　　Round us richly spread—
It's a beautiful life for a seamaid
　　On the ocean bed.
It's a beautiful life for a seamaid
　　On the ocean bed.

(*The song develops into a dance, in which* Mermen *join. Eventually they come back to the chorus*)

  Nimble little seamaids,
   Diving through the waves,
  Round we go, playing what d'ye know,
   In the green sea caves.
  If sailors on the water
   Could live below instead
  There'd be plenty more fun for a seamaid
   On the ocean bed.
  Swimming, diving,
   Little hearts aglow,
  Singing songs the Sirens sang
   A million years ago—
  If scientists of England
   Could hear our minstrelsy,
  There'd be plenty of fun for a student
   Of biology.

(*When everything has settled down again* Porpoise *rushes on*)

Porpoise. Neptune! My Lord!

(*Enter* Neptune)

Neptune.   How now? How went your quest?

Porpoise.
 Approaching swiftly from the nor'-nor'-west,
 The Saucy Alice, sailing sou'-sou'-east,
 Crosses this spot six secs from now at least.
Neptune.
 Peace to these revels! Gather swift about—
 Whirlwind, Typhoon, and ghastly Waterspout!

  "Arise!" (Neptune and Chorus)

 Arise! Arise! Arise!
 Ye dread subaqueous storms!
The Storms (*arising from behind rocks, and entering at various places*) Master!
Neptune. Ye Storms!
Storms.   Master!
Neptune.
 Ye dread subaqueous storms!
 Give ear!
Storms.   We're here!
Neptune.
 Give ear! Give ear! Give ear! Give ear! Give ear!
Storms.
 We're here, we're here!
Neptune.
 Somewhere above—upon the tranquil bosom of the deep
 A ship—

STORMS. A ship!
NEPTUNE.
  A ship doth her appointed mission keep.
  Forthwith arise! Arise! Arise! Arise! Arise!
  And toss the ocean to the darkling skies!
STORMS.
  Aha!
NEPTUNE.
  Cause ye a tempest!
STORMS.   A tempest! A tempest!
NEPTUNE.
  Stormbirds rave!
STORMS.   Rave!
NEPTUNE.
  Sink me that vessel neath the inky wave!
CHORUS.
  Cause ye a tempest!
    A tempest! A tempest!
NEPTUNE.
  Stormbirds rave! Sink me that vessel
  Neath the inky wave. Arise!
ALL.
  Arise! Arise! Arise!

(*The aria develops into a wild and sinister ballet, the light grows dim, the festoons of seaweed are agitated. Finally, on a great orchestral clash, the sea creatures run off laughing exultantly. Where machinery for such a manœuvre exists, bits of "The Saucy Alice" may float down from above. The music changes to an "after the storm" theme, the lights restore the scene to its former beauties—and* DICK, PUSS *and* CICELY *enter, looking about them in amazement—* DICK *a little ahead of the others*)

DICK.
  O, look, Dame Suett, at this lovely place!
  It must be Fairy Snowflake's magic grace
  That brings us safely here, unharmed, all three,
  Saved from the wrath of that appalling sea—
  Our garments dry, though soaked in water seething.
CICELY.
  And, which is more remarkable, still breathing.
DICK.
  I've always craved adventure, longed to peep
  At the mysterious kingdom of the deep—
  To fight with sharks, or, in some cavern hid,
  Rescue a mermaid from the giant squid.
CICELY.
  If you enjoy adventures, Dick, you've got 'em—
  But, O! the splendours of the ocean's bottom,

These iridescent shells that gleam and glister,
These pearly grottoes and that coral vista!
A sumptuous palace, yet a home from home,
All realized in gorgeous polychrome.
Dick.
And look, Dame Suett, in this ancient trunk,
The treasures of some noble ship long sunk,
Here's bags of gold, and jewels, sack on sack;
We shall be millionaires when we get back,
And then—O, then—all our misfortunes past—
My lovely Alice shall be mine at last.
Cicely.
If we were home, my boy, and on dry land,
Those words would be a signal to the band—
"My lovely Alice"—cue for song and dance—
And, crikey! What an unexpected chance!
It is not often, as you must agree,
One finds a grand piano in the sea.
Sing on! While I, with eager expectation
Conduct a little private exploration.

(*Exit* Cicely)

17. "My Lovely Alice (Dick and Sea Nymphs)

Dick.

My lovely Alice!
A thousand miles divide us—
And London city
Claims all your charming graces.
My lovely Alice!
Though fellowship's denied us,
What e'er you do
My heart's with you
And all your love embraces.

(*The* Sea Nymphs *have stolen in behind him*)

Sea Nymphs.

O lovely Alice!
A thousand miles divide you.
In Neptune's kingdom
No chance against our graces.
O Lovely Alice!
For ever love's denied you—
What e'er he will
We'll hold him still
Within our cold embraces.

Dick.
　　　　　　　　　My lovely Alice!
Sea Nymphs (*going*)
　　　　　　　　Alice! Alice! Alice!
Dick.
　　　　　　Alice!

(*Enter* Cicely)

Cicely. There you are. Did you have a nice song?

Dick. Yes, Dame Suett—but there seemed to be voices echoing me—mocking me—saying I'd never get back to London and Alice—that I'd have to stay here for ever. It was terrible—and I thought I saw figures gliding behind the rocks—but there was never anyone there when I looked.

Cicely. That proves it was all your fancy. I didn't see anyone. Not even a halibut.

Dick. That sort of fish doesn't live down here. If we meet anything it will be some sort of monster.

Cicely. Oh, nonsense! I don't believe in the terrors of the deep. The whole thing's an old have invented by divers. Sharks! Ha ha! I don't believe in 'em.

(*A* Shark *passes across behind them, from one cave to another*)

Dick. I don't believe in mermaids and Neptune and all that stuff, Dame Suett—but there *are* sharks.

Cicely. I haven't seen any.

(Shark *passes back again*)

I suppose you'll be telling me next you believe in the sea serpent.

Dick. I don't know about that.

Cicely. I should think not. Just a sailor's yarn to make them out more interesting people than they really are. Sea serpent indeed! I'll sea serpent 'em!

(*The face of the* Sea Serpent *peers out of a grotto*)

Dick. I'll give you the sea serpent, Dame Suett.

Cicely. Thanks very much.

(Sea Serpent *withdraws*)

Dick. But you must believe in squids—the giant octopus.

Cicely. Octopus! What's that? Cat with eight lives?

Puss. Wow!

Dick. It's all very well to laugh, Dame Suett—but we've got to look out.

Cicely. All right, my boy; *you* go and look out—and let me have a nice rest on this agreeable marine settee.

Dick. Very good, Dame Suett. There's an old sword in this treasure chest. If anything attacks us, I'll let it have it. One, two, three, wallop! Eh? Death of the giant squid! Hooray!

Cicely. All right, Dick; run along and find your old squid, and let me have my rest.

Dick. Come on, Puss!

(*Exeunt* Dick *and* Puss)

Cicely. A nice boy. But very nervous. I've walked all round and there's absolutely nothing in sight at all. Now I ask you—do you see anything? If you do, let me know. Just shout out "Hi!" Let's have a little rehearsal, shall we? One, two, three——

Audience. Hi!

Cicely. *That* won't do. I'd never hear you if I was asleep. Try again. One, two, three——

Audience. Hi!

Cicely. That's better. Don't forget. If you see anything, shout out quickly. And say *what* it is and *where*. Hi! Sea serpent! or Hi! Shark! or Hi! Squid! I shall be *so* much obliged to you.

(Sea Serpent *peeps out*)

Audience. Hi! Sea serpent!

Cicely (*looking the wrong way*) What? Where?

Audience. On your right!

(Sea Serpent *retires*)

Cicely. I don't see anything.

(Shark *peeps out on the other side*)

Audience. Hi! Shark!

Cicely. Oh! Where? What?

Audience. On the other side!

(Shark *retires*)

Cicely. Now, that's really very naughty of you. I shan't believe a word you say if you tease me like that. I'll forgive you this time. I like a joke as well as anyone—but don't do it again. I'm just going to have a nice doze.

(17A. *Orchestra plays "Rockaby Baby"*, Cicely *settles down on her settee. From a dark grotto (or from the chest) the* Giant Squid *emerges and slowly approaches*)

Audience. Look out! Hi! The squid!

Cicely. Oh no—you don't have me on three times.

(*The* Squid *gets nearer and puts an arm on* Cicely. *She brushes it off*)

One trouble about being under the sea is the seaweed.

(Squid *puts arm round her neck*)

Is that you, Dick? Back already?

(SQUID *puts another arm round neck*)

I must say you're very affectionate all of a sudden. Did you see anything? Any mermaids or squids? What's the matter with you, eh? Can't you answer? (*Slowly she becomes aware that all is not well*) Aaaaaah! Help! Dick! (*She jumps away and dashes across towards the opposite grotto*)

(*The* SEA SERPENT *emerges. Melodrama music ad lib.* CICELY *rushes the other way. The* SHARK *appears. She turns back and finds herself faced by the* SQUID. *The* SQUID *chases her.* DICK *and* PUSS *enter.* DICK *tackles the* SQUID, *fencing with his sword.* CICELY *fences with her umbrella.* PUSS *boxes the* SEA SERPENT. *The* SQUID *gets an arm round both* DICK *and* CICELY. *It looks like the end. The chase is one of the oldest of pantomime traditions, originally including a deal of trap work. The extent of this entertainment can only be worked out in production. Enter* NEPTUNE, *and train of* MERMEN. *Grand chord*)

NEPTUNE.
    Hoho! Dick Whittington—we call your bluff.
    You don't believe in Neptune and such stuff.
    Lobsters and lampreys! If your skill so much is—
    Why don't you 'scape from Neptune's royal clutches?
MERMEN (*closing in menacingly*)
    Why don't you 'scape from Neptune's royal clutches?
DICK.
    Against your evil, in this desperate hour,
    I set the might of Fairy Snowflake's power—
    Oppose to yours her word of magic lore,
    "Love is the key that opens every door!"

(*Swirl of music. Powder flash.* FAIRY SNOWFLAKE *appears, either entering from the* R, *or, more dramatically, through a trick door in a coral grotto*)

SNOWFLAKE.
    Well said, brave Dick! Your touching faith in me
    Brings you assistance, even in the sea.
NEPTUNE.
    Scallops and squids! What bodes this intervention?
SNOWFLAKE.
    It bodes, King Neptune, that your vile intention
    To drown this lad, this cat, this honest dame,
    Shall ring through history as a deed of shame.
    Lucky for you, Dick, by my magic art
    I watched *The Saucy Alice* from the start,
    And, warned of danger in this hostile sea,
    Made haste to gain my fairy pharmacy,

Where I concocted—for the need was urgent—
A novel and miraculous detergent,
One pinch of which amid the ocean's brine
Shall render powerless these foes of thine.

(SNOWFLAKE *scatters something. Musical phrase. The* CREATURES
retire in confusion. NEPTUNE *staggers*)

NEPTUNE.
Conger and crabs!
SNOWFLAKE.   No swearing, if you please!
Your claims are forfeit to control the seas,
No longer shall mankind be Neptune's slaves
From this time forth Britannia rules the waves.

(NEPTUNE *utters a howl—which is smothered by the first phrase of*
"*Rule Britannia*". BRITANNIA *descends in a bathysphere, and steps
down. Or the bathysphere can come in from the side if a descent is
difficult*)

SNOWFLAKE.
Welcome, Britannia—
BRITANNIA.   Welcome kindred soul!
Passing this way upon routine patrol,
Your splendid words I chanced to overhear,
And hastened hither in my bathysphere.
In cause of justice never known to fail,
Can my assistance anyway avail?
Eager as ever, dear, to intervene,
What can I do to keep the ocean clean?
SNOWFLAKE.
Just this, dear madam, with your kind connivance,
Transport my friends in your unique contrivance,
No matter if a trifle chocko-blocko,
And land them on the coast of old Morocco.
BRITANNIA.
A service, madam, I will gladly render,
And as for you, King Neptune, vile offender,
Back to your basic mud and there remain!
Nor dare to touch an Englishman again!

(*Exit* NEPTUNE *and* MERMEN)

DICK.
Thank you, good Fairy, for your kindly aid.
SNOWFLAKE.
Love called, dear boy, and love must be obeyed.
And now go forward, 'neath that lucky star,
To meet your destiny in Africa.

DICK.
But where, good madam?
SNOWFLAKE.   Ask not where, or when
Such things are hid, my dear, from mortal ken.
This only you are privileged to know:
The wretch who plots your daily overthrow
Is called King Rat.
DICK.   King Rat!
SNOWFLAKE.   A faithless rodent—
Supreme in villainy, in foulness potent.
Seek out this infamy, this fiend abase,
And earn the plaudits of the human race.
BRITANNIA (*standing by the bathysphere*) Going up!
SNOWFLAKE.
But come! I hear my sailor colleague murmur
'Tis time to set your course for *terra firma*.
Don't fail to help yourselves to Neptune's treasure.
CICELY.
A thousand thanks, Ma'am.
SNOWFLAKE.   Not at all: a pleasure.
And so, farewell! Aboard! But never fear!
All those who hold my fairy maxim dear,
Shall find that even on Morocco's shore
Love is the key that opens every door.

(*The* SEA NYMPHS *and* MERMEN *steal on and lend their voices as*
DICK, CICELY *and* PUSS *climb into the bathysphere, waving to*
FAIRY SNOWFLAKE)

ALL.
                    That opens every door—
                    Ah me!
                    That opens every door—
                    Love is the key, the sesame,
                    That opens every door.

                    CURTAIN

ACT III

Prologue

Scene—*Before the prologue cloth.*

Enter Fairy Snowflake.

Snowflake.
    Just as I hoped! The bell rings—you obey—
    Eager to watch the progress of our play.
    Be sure, my dears, I blame you not at all
    For seeking something in the interval.
    In thrilling scenes where Honour strives with Hate
    The nervous strain is really much too great,
    And very rightly we implore the aid
    Of a refreshing glass of lemonade.
    Act Two was certainly a narrow squeak!
    Poor Cicely was nearly up the creek.
    But trust Britannia to deserve her laurels
    And make a powerful stand for decent morals.
    She'll teach those sharks to sing a note less strident,
    And show old Neptune where to put his trident.
    And, even now, her excellent machine
    Conveys our hero to th' ensuing scene
    Where, I must warn you, there is like to be
    A dreadful struggle with Impiety.
    When days are dark, and courage at the ebb,
    Evil, like some vile spider, spins his web.
    But never doubt! Ere it can dim Life's lustre,
    Comes Love, hey presto! with his little duster.
    E'en so, in this periculous affair,
    I'll trust Dick Whittington to do and dare.
    Let locksmiths argue and my words deplore,
    I still believe Love opens every door.

(*Music*)

    But hark! Soft music through the aether winning
    Shows that Act Three is just about beginning.
    We shan't be late; for see! By magic taught
    (*She waves her wand*)
    The curtain rises on the Sultan's court.

(*Exit* Snowflake)

SCENE I

SCENE—*An arcaded courtyard of the Sultan's Palace.*

In the C *the* SULTAN *sits upon a pile of silken cushions. On either side stand slaves and officers of state, among them the* CHIEF EUNUCH *of the* MASTER OF THE HOUSEHOLD. GIRLS OF THE HAREM *are dancing.*

18. "EI! WALLAH! WALLAH! WALLAH!" (HAREM GIRLS)

GIRLS OF THE HAREM.

Ei! Wallah, wallah, wallah!
Ei! Wallah, wallah, wallah!
Ei! Wallah, wallah, wallah!
Ei! Wallah, wallah, wallah!
Clang, clang, clang!
Ah! Ah!

I

All like a summer dream,
  Girls of thy harem;
Slender or broad of beam,
  Girls of thy harem.
Raise then thy comely voice,
Make then thy evening choice,
  Lord of the harem!
  Lord of the harem!
Ei! Wallah, wallah, wallah!
Ei! Wallah, wallah, wallah!
Ei! Wallah, wallah, wallah!
Ei! Wallah, wallah, wallah!
Clang, clang, clang!
Ah! Ah!

II

Roses surround thy bed,
  Lord of the harem—
Why hangest thou thy head
  Lord of the harem?
Far-famed voluptuary,
Why this austerity,
  Lord of the harem?
Ei! Wallah, wallah, wallah!
Ei! Wallah, wallah, wallah!
Ei! Wallah, wallah, wallah!
Ei! Wallah, wallah, wallah!
Clang, clang, clang!
Ah! Ah!

III

> All like a summer dream
>   Girls of thy harem;
> Slender or broad of beam,
>   Girls of thy harem—
> Can we not rouse in thee
>   Any cupidity,
>   Lord of the harem?

Sultan. Away!
Girls.

> Ei! Wallah, wallah, wallah!
> Ei! Wallah, wallah, wallah!
> Ei! Wallah, wallah, wallah!
> Clang, clang, clang!

(*The disappointed* Girls *have withdrawn*)

Sultan. Summon the Chief Eunuch!
Master of the Household (*after blowing a whistle*) Summon the Chief Eunuch!
Slaves. Summon the Chief Eunuch!
Sultan. Come hither, thou son of mischance.
Chief Eunuch. May Your Majesty honour me with commands!
Sultan. Have any ships been captured on the Barbary Coast these six weeks?
Chief Eunuch. I believe not, Your Majesty.
Sultan. Have any Christian maidens been washed up on my hospitable shores these six months?
Chief Eunuch. I regret, Your Majesty—no.
Sultan. Why not?
Chief Eunuch. Your Majesty's humble ser——
Sultan. Do I not need slaves? Is not my harem lamentably understocked? For half a year I have seen the same faces smirking at me, the same torsos waggling at me, the same—but I will not enumerate the whole dismal catalogue. I am sick of the lot of them.
Chief Eunuch. I have searched the country, Your Majesty. There do not appear to be any maidens, who have not already been rejected by the wisdom of your exalted experience. The shores have been watched night and day. No Christians have been washed up.
Sultan. I do not care what you have searched and where you have watched. Where is your success? Find me a new distraction or I will have you nailed to the city gates.
Chief Eunuch. Yes, Your Majesty.
Sultan. Or possibly sawn in half. I will consider the matter and let you know. Be gone.

(*Exit the* Chief Eunuch)

E

Summon the Master of the Household!

Master of the Household (*after blowing his whistle*) Summon the Master of the Household!

Slaves. Summon the Master of the Household!

Master of the Household. Oh! that's me.

Sultan. Make your report. I have no doubt that you have carried out all my commands.

Master of the Household. Yes, Your Majesty.

Sultan. That is well.

Master of the Household. Excepting only in one respect——

Sultan. Ah!

Master of the Household. Alas! Your Majesty, it is no fault of mine, but I have ill news——

Sultan. Ill news!

Master of the Household. Yes, Your Majesty.

Sultan. Speak on. I cannot devise the details of your punishment until I know the extent of your failure.

Master of the Household. It is the rats, Your Majesty.

Sultan. Rats!

Master of the Household. Yes, Your Majesty.

Sultan. I gave orders that they should be expelled from my dominions a month ago.

Master of the Household. Yes, Your Majesty. But they will not go.

Sultan. Will not!

Master of the Household. No, Your Majesty. They are gathering in the palace cellars in battalions. I have locked all the doors. I have shouted your orders through every keyhole. But they will not go. I have given them food to help them on their journey. Still they will not go. I have placed traps but they will not enter them. Now they are gnawing holes in the floors, and at any time I fear they will advance and occupy the whole palace.

Sultan. Go, dolt, and order our bodyguard to stand with swords drawn to defend our person.

Master of the Household. The creatures are so many and so nimble, Your Majesty, that I fear they will penetrate such defences. I would entreat you to remove to another of Your Majesty's cities.

Sultan. And leave the palace to be ratsacked! Away! Do as I command!

Master of the Household. As Your Majesty wills . . . Oh dear!

(*Exit* Master of the Household)

Sultan. By the beard of the Prophet! Was ever monarch so plagued by incompetent servants? Too many rats—not enough women!

(*Enter a* Servant)

Well—what is it?

Servant. The Warden of Your Majesty's Coasts requests audience. He has prisoners with him, sir.

Sultan. Prisoners! At last! Bring them in. This may divert my mind from the anxieties of existence. Bring them in.

(*Enter the* Warden *with* Dick, *shackled,* Cicely, *veiled, and* Puss, *on a chain*)

You are welcome, Warden. What have we here?

Warden. These two persons, Your Majesty, male and female, and this extraordinary animal was seen approaching off Your Majesty's coast last night at three o'clock by my pocket hourglass, in a mysterious vessel, what landed them upon the shore and then withdrew. Taking them for unlawful spies I apprehended them and brought them at once to Your Majesty's court, having first taken the precaution of covering the female prisoner who was walking unveiled upon Your Majesty's earth, like the shameless hussy that she undoubtedly is.

Cicely. I'll have you know, young man . . .

Warden. Silence!

Sultan. H'm—the man looks strong. He may go to the galleys.

Dick. Your Majesty . . .

Sultan. And this animal may, perhaps, be placed in the Royal Menagerie.

Puss. Wow!

Dick. Your Majesty! May I speak?

Sultan. It is not usual. But you may.

Dick. We are no spies, Your Majesty, but English visitors to your shores.

Sultan. English visitors! You surprise me. Where is your knitting and your paintbox?

Dick. We *are* English, sir, I assure you—and if we can be of service, we will gladly strive to please you. But I beg you not to arrest us. I ask your help. I am seeking an enemy, who, I have reason to believe, is hiding in these parts.

Sultan. An enemy?

Dick. And my cat, Your Majesty—please don't put him in a menagerie.

Puss. Wow!

Dick. Puss is a splendid fellow, and the best rat-catcher in the world, aren't you, Puss?

Puss. Wow!

Sultan. Rat-catcher! Rat-catcher! In the holy name of Akbar, I have an immediate service for you. Master of the Household!

Slaves. Master of the Household!

(*Enter* Master of the Household)

E*

MASTER OF THE HOUSEHOLD. Your Majesty!

SULTAN. Take this man and this animal and admit them to the Palace vaults.

MASTER OF THE HOUSEHOLD. The vaults, Your Majesty! They will be eaten alive.

SULTAN. If they are, so be it. But if they succeed in defeating these infidel rats they will earn the greatest reward my gratitude can offer. Understand this, young man. My kingdom is plagued with rats. If you wish to win your liberty, if you can trust your courage and your cat's ability—then there is your service.

DICK. And I and Puss will gladly undertake it, sir.

PUSS. Wow!

DICK. Give me my sword. It may well be that your enemy and mine are one and the same villain. Lead on!

SULTAN. Take them away.

(*Exeunt* DICK, PUSS *and the* MASTER OF THE HOUSEHOLD)

The Court is dismissed. You will be rewarded, Warden.

WARDEN. I thank Your Majesty.

SULTAN. At our future convenience.

WARDEN. And the woman, Your Majesty?

SULTAN. Take her to the slaves' quarters.

CICELY. The *what?*

WARDEN. Silence! Come on.

(*The* SULTAN *glances after them, and is suddenly transfixed by the sight of Cicely's back view*)

SULTAN. One moment. I will speak with this woman. Leave us.

(*Exeunt the* WARDEN *and other members of the Sultan's suite*)

H'm. I have not seen your face, but I find you well-favoured and rounded in a manner that is new to my experience.

CICELY. Ooo! The things Your Majesty says!

SULTAN. Remove your veil.

CICELY. Oh—I couldn't.

SULTAN. Remove your veil.

CICELY. No, really. Really, I couldn't.

SULTAN. Remove your veil.

CICELY. Well—as Your Majesty pleases. I hope you won't be disappointed.

SULTAN. Disappointed! Disappointed! Such beauty stuns me.

CICELY. You mean, Your Majesty likes little me?

SULTAN. I do mean it. You shall become a member of my exalted harem.

CICELY. Oh! I couldn't, sir. Really, I couldn't.

SULTAN. Certainly you could. It is not difficult. Come—let me teach thee.

CICELY. Ooo! Your Majesty—I hope Your Majesty's intentions are strictly honourable.

SULTAN. Honourable as night, my gentle gazelle.

CICELY. I'm glad to hear it. For a moment I thought——

SULTAN. Think nothing, O moon of loveliness, except that I am as a refreshing well, sunk in the deserts of an arid and contrary existence. Will you not quench your thirst? Will you not rest beneath the overshadowing branches of my inordinate affection?

CICELY. Well, of course, Your Majesty . . . if you put it that way . . .

19. "GENTLE DESERT FAIRY" (SULTAN and CICELY)

I

SULTAN.

Gentle desert fairy,
Halt your dromedary
By the green oasis of my heart.
Desert sands are parching,
Here are palm trees arching
In the green oasis of my heart.
Underneath the verdant bough
With a jug of wine and thou,
Crooning near me, all the world apart,
In the Desert of Desire
You're the girl that I require
In the green oasis of my heart.

II

CICELY.

Other girls may hanker
After Casablanca,
Ever more I'll stay beside my man.
I'm not going places
From this old oasis,
Here I mean to park my caravan.
For a palace life I trow
Is a paradise enow—
From your side I'll never never part.
In the Desert of Desire
You're the man that I require
In the green oasis of my heart.

(*The two dance to a repeat of the first half of the tune, returning to sing the second half in duet*)

SULTAN *and* CICELY.

For a palace life I trow
Will be paradise with thou—

From your side I'll never, never part.
In the Desert of Desire
You're the one that I require
In the green oasis of my heart.

SCENE 2

SCENE—*The Palace Vaults.*

Enter DICK *cautiously, sword in hand. He whips round and peers behind him.*

DICK (*in a hoarse whisper*) Who's there? I could have sworn I heard someone following me. I think one hears the echo of one's own footsteps. Nothing seems stirring—and yet maybe every hole and cranny in these mouldering walls shelters an enemy. Psst! What's that? There is someone yonder—coming this way. I'll hide and watch.

(*Exit* R, *as* KING RAT *enters from the* L)

KING RAT.
My dirty machinations move apace;
The Saucy Alice sunk without a trace,
Foul Whittington and his accursed cat
Gone to old Neptune—what d'you think of that?
Drowned without mercy in the flaming sea—
A masterpiece of black diplomacy!
That wretch destroyed, the Rodent flag unfurled
Shall wave triumphant o'er a prostrate world,
Wherein, the climax to my Five-Year Plan,
The place of shame shall be reserved for Man,
Holes in the wall his refuge from my hate,
While Rats divide the offices of state.
Rats in the Treasury, a long-felt wish,
Rats in the Ministry of Ag. and Fish.
Everywhere Rodents, growing rich and fat,
And all subservient to me—King Rat.

(*Enter* DICK)

DICK.
King Rat! So there you are!
KING RAT.   Who calls my name?
Death and damnation! Whittington!
DICK.   The same—
Saved by a miracle from that dread sea,
And here to try conclusions, Rat, with thee.
KING RAT.
Mouse! Pigmy! Midget! Grub! Pestiferous Mite!
Dost think that *thou* canst save the cause of Right?

Down in the cellars, fifty thousand strong,
My Rodents wait to hail the Age of Wrong.

DICK.
And long they'll wait, King Rat. Unknown to fear,
E'en now my cat attacks them in the rear.

KING RAT.
Pest on your cat! My All-Victorious Vermin
His nine detested lives shall soon determine,
What time this blade shall purge thy dire offence—
And then—Whack-ho! for Vice and Crapulence!

(19A. FIGHT MUSIC. *An exciting fight with swords—in which* KING
RAT *appears to be getting the best of it. They have got themselves over
on the left side of the scene*)

What-ho! Dick Whittington—you tire, you tire!
Where is your rapier's grace, your youthful fire?
Come, yield to me!

DICK.
                              Love never yields to hate.

KING RAT.
Speak not of Love, boy. You appeal too late!

(*A sudden blow knocks the sword from Dick's hand.* DICK *falls on one
knee*)

What can avail you now, homunculus?

DICK.
One thing alone—hey! To the rescue! Puss!

(KING RAT *is bending down ready to make a final thrust, when* PUSS
*lands on his back in a flying leap from the wings. Clash of music. To
loud music a roughhouse develops between* PUSS *and* KING RAT—*from
which* RAT *emerges screaming with terror, and escapes on his own side
of the stage. Good comic business can be made of this fight.* RAT *can
be chased over the footlights and through the auditorium. When the
excitement is over* PUSS *sits down and washes his ears*)

Dear Puss! The Fairy's love beneath the sea
Saved us from that foul fiend's malignancy.
Here I had perished but for your brave claw—
Yours was the love that oped my prison door.
Come on! We'll claim a fortune with this story—
And then—sing hey for Alice, Home, and Glory!

(*They march off stage* R, *extremely pleased with themselves*)

Scene 3

Scene—*The Palace.*

When the Curtain *rises the* Girls *are dancing, and the* Court
Officials *and* Slaves *in position. The Sultan's place is empty.*

20. "Sound the Jolly Plectrum"

(Slaves, Court Officials, Girls etc.)

Chorus.
> Sound the jolly plectrum, marimba, and sackbut!
> Make a merry music with timbrel and drums!
> Near was our destruction from rodent attack but
> Now a song of triumph our voices becomes.
> Now a song of triumph our voices becomes.
>> So—graceful and nimble,
>> We sway to the cymbal,
>> In artless Arabian fashion,
>> In hopes of arousing,
>> Mid joyful carousing,
> Some thoughts of the tenderer passion.
> Swing a jolly pelvis in movement ecstatic!
> Twist a merry torso in dancing and song!
> Bang a happy elbow with tambour emphatic!
> Welcome our defender with cymbal and gong!
>> Swing a jolly pelvis!
>> Twist a merry torso!
> Sound the jolly cymbal, marimba, and gong!

(Near the end of this Chorus the Sultan *has entered holding* Dick *by
the hand, and* Puss *by the other hand. They sit down in the prepared
places in the centre of the scene)*

Sultan. Well, Master of the Household, I hope for your sake
that you have a better report to make than you had earlier in
the day.

Master of the Household. I have indeed, sir. Your Majesty's
kingdom is now entirely free from rats. Twenty-four thousand,
three hundred and nine were slain in the cellar by Master
Whittington's remarkable cat. The remaining twenty-five
thousand, six hundred and ninety-one have fled in the direction
of the sea. Their abominable leader, severely mauled, was last seen
fleeing in the direction of Tangier.

Sultan. Master Whittington, you and your noble cat have
earned our gratitude. You shall be rewarded.

*(*Puss *rubs against the* Sultan, *and the* Sultan *strokes him)*

Dick. I thank Your Majesty.

Sultan. I offer you, Master Whittington, any five of the beautiful damsels that grace my court.

Dick. Your Majesty is very generous and very thoughtful—but one girl alone absorbs my love. I want none other.

Sultan. What an astonishing thing! You English are a remarkable race. I don't understand you at all. You would prefer to take your reward in money, I suppose.

Dick. If you please, sir.

Sultan. I feared you would. Seventy-five thousand pounds, I have been told, is the natural aim of every normal Englishman. That sum shall be paid to you.

Dick. I thank Your Majesty.

Sultan. I would be very happy if you would stay with me, Whittington.

Dick. You are kind, sir—but my heart is in London. I would be a poor sort of creature if I did not follow it.

Sultan. And Puss? Will he stay?

Puss. Wa-wow-wow-*wa*!

Sultan. Where is *his* heart?

Dick. I rather think it's in England, too, sir. He has a friend—at Highgate, I believe.

Puss. Prrr! Wow!

Sultan. So be it, my noble friends. I can oppose you in nothing. But there will still be one link between us. The fair Cicely has agreed to stay with me—and to become one of my happy family of laughing girls. Come, Master of the Household! What are you waiting for?

Master of the Household. Your Majesty . . .

Sultan. Command our ballet, dolt—and let it be stimulating, oscillating, and undulating—or I will have you sawn in half, lengthways.

Master of the Household. As Your Majesty pleases. (*He claps his hands*)

(20A. *The* Girls *begin to dance. Part way through, to the barbaric clash of cymbals,* Cicely *enters and dances the part of première danseuse, to the great delight of the* Sultan)

SCENE 4

Scene—*A London Street.*

Enter Fairy Snowflake.

Snowflake.
　　I couldn't be more pleased. The plan was bold
　　But worked precisely as the stars foretold.
　　And now with Mars and Saturn in conjunction,
　　Venus performing her familiar function,

The Dog-star setting and the Moon ascending,
I think we must achieve a happy ending.
E'en now Dick makes his way to old Fitzwarren's,
Weighted with golden guineas, silver florins,
Eager to summon Justice to his side,
To clear his name and claim a lovely bride.
Which things accomplished, 'twill be only fair
If he's elected to be London's mayor.

(*Enter* King Rat. *He has a bandage round his head, his arm in a sling; and is limping*)

King Rat.
    Foiled once again! For, hid behind the scenes,
    I heard you, as per usual, spill the beans.
Snowflake.
    Really, King Rat, for all your wonted gall,
    You look more fitted for the hospital.
    Have you been in the wars since last we met?
King Rat.
    Mock not, vile Snowflake! You shall suffer yet!
    For every scratch, each torturing contusion,
    Your Dick shall pay a frightful retribution.
Snowflake.
    Pernicious thing! At this stage in Act Three
    It's much too late for fresh chicanery.
    You would not hark when I proclaimed before
    That Love had power to open *every* door:
    Find now, King Rat, to your eternal rue
    One door that opens specially for you!

(Snowflake *waves her wand at* King Rat's *feet. Powder-flash. He suddenly disappears down the trap in a billow of red smoke; or, if no trap, through a flap in the scenery*)

King Rat. Hi-yi!
Snowflake.
    Thank goodness that it worked! Had it not been
    That Uranus, a planet rarely seen,
    Is at this hour conjunct with mighty Saturn,
    Fate might have drawn a very different pattern.
    I dread to think—but there! The danger's past
    And Love shall crown our enterprise at last.

(*Music*)

    But come! Sweet Alice waits—so no more parley.
    We'll meet again, dears, at the Grand Finale.

Scene 5

Scene—*Alderman Fitzwarren's Parlour.*
Enter Simon.

Simon. Mistress Alice!

(*Enter* Alice)

Alice. Yes, Simon.

Simon. That there Marmaduke's down below. He says he's expected, Miss.

Alice. Yes, Simon. And my father and Alderman Bung will be here too, in a minute. They are determined to force me into marriage.

Simon. Mistress Alice, we're all sorry for you——

Alice. Dear Simon!

Simon. But we do know that the ship went down with all hands, Miss——

Alice. Don't, Simon.

Simon. I only meant, Miss——

Alice. Yes, Simon, I know. Thank you for all your kindness. Show Master Marmaduke up.

Simon. Yes, Miss.

(*Exit* Simon)

Alice. I will never consent. If it should come to the last—I'll kill myself—I swear I will.

(*Exit* r Alice.
    Enter l Marmaduke, *absurdly dressed for an important occasion*)

Marmaduke. Sweet Mistress Alice! What? Not here? Expectation of today's delight hath turned my mind, which was never one of the strongest, into a whirligig. To think that ere another hour has passed I shall be betrothed! My heart is like a singing bird . . .

21. "Alice Where Art Thou?" (Marmaduke)

Marmaduke.

Alice, where art thou?
  In thy downy nest,
List to the music
  Bubbling in this breast.
Birds of the greenwood
  Raise their carol true
Cuckoo!
Jug-jug!
Poo-wheeeeeeee!
Tu-whitawoo!

(*Enter* Alderman Bung)

BUNG. That's my brave boy. Serenading your loved one?

MARMADUKE. Yes, Father. Let us call her again. You help. You be jug-jug. And I'll be the cuckoo.

BUNG. I think that is very probable, my boy.

(*The song is repeated in duet*)

MARMADUKE *and* BUNG.
>Alice, where art thou?
>In thy downy nest,
>List to the music
>>Bubbling in this breast.
>Birds of the greenwood
>>Raise their carol true
>Cuckoo!
>Jug-jug!
>Poo-wheeeeeeee!
>Tu-whitawoo!

(*Enter* ALDERMAN FITZWARREN)

FITZWARREN. Ah, good sire! You have stolen a march on me. You are serenading my Alice—my little daughter.

FITZWARREN. Come—let us call her all together.

BUNG. An excellent idea. You be poo-whee, good sir. I will be jug-jug.

MARMADUKE. And I will be the cuckoo.

FITZWARREN. I should think that would be very probable, my boy.

(*They sing as a trio, and with considerable elaboration*)

MARMADUKE, BUNG *and* FITZWARREN.
>Alice, where art thou?
>>In thy downy nest,
>List to the music
>>Bubbling in this breast.
>Birds of the greenwood
>>Raise their carol true
>Cuckoo!
>Jug-jug!
>Poo-wheeeeeeee!
>Tu-whitawoo!

Come forth, Alice!

(ALICE *enters*)

ALICE. Good morning, Father. Good morning, gentlemen.

FITZWARREN. Today it is, my child, that we have agreed to celebrate your betrothal with our good friend and neighbour, Master Marmaduke—one who will love and care for you and keep you in that state of life to which your position justly entitles you——

(*Enter* SIMON)

SIMON. Sir!

FITZWARREN. What is the meaning of this intrusion?

(*Enter* SALLY)

SALLY. Master!

FITZWARREN. Eh? What's this?

SALLY. He's back, sir!

FITZWARREN. Who is, girl?

SIMON. Dick, sir.

SALLY. Dick Whittington.

ALICE. Dick Whittington!

MARMADUKE. Whittington!

FITZWARREN. And what of it? We want no thieves here. What signifies it if Master Whittington does return?

ALICE. It signifies this, sir. I will not wed with Master Marmaduke. I will only wed where my heart dictates.

BUNG. Surely, Master Fitzwarren, you will not put up with this insubordination?

FITZWARREN. Certainly not, Master Bung. Alice, if you will not wed Master Marmaduke, you shall go straight into a nunnery. This is a rich and eligible match. I demand your obedience. This may be the fourteenth century—the age of progress. But we have not progressed so far that a child shall flout her father to his face. Obey at once, you baggage, or——

(*Enter* DICK)

DICK. You must forgive my interrupting you, Master Fitzwarren . . .

ALICE. Dick!

DICK. Alice!

FITZWARREN. How dare you, sir!

MARMADUKE. This is an outrage!

DICK. I know, Alderman, that I ought not to burst in upon you in this manner. But there is something you do not know—something you must know.

FITZWARREN. Indeed, sir?

DICK. I am rich, sir. Extremely rich.

FITZWARREN. You are what, sir!

DICK. Rich—rich beyond anything this city has ever known.

FITZWARREN. Oh . . .

DICK. You see my argument, sir, I am sure.

FITZWARREN. I do, sir.

BUNG. I warn you, Alderman, not to listen to this dangerous fellow.

Fitzwarren. On the contrary, Master Bung, I am surprised that you should take such an unreasonable attitude. Ever since I heard of the false accusation——

Marmaduke. False accusation!

Fitzwarren. Which was preferred against Master Whittington by this, this, by your son, Master Bung——

Bung. Sir!

Fitzwarren. I have felt gravely disturbed in mind. The proof was incomplete. It should not have been accepted. In the circumstances I have decided to bestow my daughter's hand on this good citizen. Take her, Master Whittington! She is yours.

Bung. Really, Master Fitzwarren!

Marmaduke. This is most unjust, sir. I have been to a great expense to purchase a new outfit against my nuptials, and now . . .

Dick. Come, Master Bung, let us have no hard words. You shall not lose by this. I have bags of money. I will give you lots of it.

Marmaduke. Will you really?

Dick. Yes, friend.

Marmaduke. Master Whittington—I am overwhelmed by your generosity. You force me to confess. It was *I* who put the money in your pocket . . .

Fitzwarren. Great heavens!

Bung. Marmaduke!

Sally. Didn't I say . . .

Simon. Well, I'll be jiggered . . .

Marmaduke. I have wronged you, Dick—but I did it for love, sir . . .

Dick. And how can I blame you for loving my lovely Alice?

21A. Reprise No. 17. "My Lovely Alice" (Ensemble)

Dick, Bung, Marmaduke and Fitzwarren.
    O lovely Alice,
    No more shall care divide {you / us.}

    For waves and mountains
    Can part a lover never
    O lovely Alice
    Soon, soon, {he'll / I'll} walk beside you
    While Old Bow Bell
    {Your / Our} wedding tells
    And makes you {mine / his} for ever.

SCENE 6

SCENE—*A London Street.*

Enter CICELY *wearing an enveloping travelling cloak, which conveniently covers her finale costume, and a sun helmet with a wisp of green trailer. She carries a huge suitcase with* SUETT, LONDON *marked on it and a few labels such as* CASABLANCA *and* TANGIER.

CICELY. If you thought I was going to stay in Morocco you were quite wrong. I couldn't stand it; really I couldn't. You'd never believe what I've gone through with that Sultan—after all his promises, too. So I packed my bag and came straight back to London. Ah well—we all make mistakes. I'd never have won fame in Morocco—not with all that competition—but in London I'm somebody. My name is already attached to a pudding, you know! That's something—eh? Dame Suett's Pudding. If you like I'll give you the recipe, free, gratis and for nothing—and also of course to allow time for all the rest of them to change their clothes for the last scene. Selfish lot they are, I don't mind telling you. What about me, I'd like to know? But I'll be even with them. That nice Fairy Snowflake has kindly given me a spell, which will change my clothes in a wink and I'll be just as grand as any of them—you see! Well—here's the secret recipe for Dame Suett's Pudding. It's got to be done to music, you know, or it doesn't come out right.

22. "EAT A LOT OF SUET" (CICELY)

CICELY.

> Now listen carefully,
> I'll tell you how to do it—
> To half a pound of flour
> Add half a pound of suet.
> Mix to a paste with a little water,
> And insert one raisin—
> Then pour the whole ghastly mess
> Into a buttered basin.
> Cover with a cloth
> And place in boiling water
> And fish it out in one hour and a quarter.
>
> Eat a lot of suet,
> Everyone should do it—
> Eat a plateful ev'ry day.
> After several pieces
> Energy increases
> In a gratifying way.

  Everybody buys it,
  Medicos advise it—
  And the doctor knows what's what—
  For there's so much good in
  Lovely suet pudding
  If you eat it hot, hot, hot.

(*Audience singing follows ad lib*)

SCENE 7

SCENE—*The Guildhall.*

Everyone arrives including the White Cat with a basket of black and white kittens—to a reprise of the most suitable music.

23. FINALE

(*When the company has assembled,* FAIRY SNOWFLAKE *advances*)

SNOWFLAKE.
  The golden test is how a story *ends*—
  And once again Right triumphs, gentle friends,
  With this vile thing accorded his release
  Only to point the moral of our piece.
  Believe me, dears, Dick's tale is not unique—
  Nor is its noble lesson far to seek.
  If each of you when evil fate attacks him
  Will have recourse to my immortal maxim,
  Yours shall be roses, roses, o'er and o'er,
  Love is the key that opens every door.

(SNOWFLAKE *retires and* DICK *and* ALICE *advance to the footlights*)

ALICE.
  Love is the key—and gladly do I pay
  Our loving thanks for your support today.
DICK.
  Good luck, old friends, throughout the coming year
  May you enjoy good courage and good cheer,
  Enough of riches, and the tender passion
  To face the world
    Shipshape and Bristol fashion.

(*And the whole company bring the pantomime to a close by singing that number*)

24. Reprise No. 14. "SHIPSHAPE AND BRISTOL FASHION"

(THE COMPANY)

CURTAIN

PROPERTY PLOT

PROLOGUE

Personal—Wand (SNOWFLAKE)

ACT I

SCENE 1

Off stage—Rolling pin (CICELY)
           Fish (CAT)
Personal—Purse (ALICE)

SCENE 3

On stage—Bales of cloth
           Tape-measure
           Outsize tailor's shears
           Safe. *In it:* money bags
           Large ledger
Off stage—Bucket, scrubbing brush (SALLY)
           Mop (SIMON)
           Dustpan and brush (CICELY)
           Fantastic Hoover (SIMON)

SCENE 5

Set as Scene 3

ACT II

SCENE 1

On stage—Barrels
           Bench
Off stage—Can of ale (MATE)
           Umbrella (CICELY)

SCENE 2

Off stage—Shopping bag (ALICE)

SCENE 3

On stage—Old chest
Off stage—Scroll (NEPTUNE)
           Box of detergent (SNOWFLAKE)

ACT III

SCENE 1

On stage—Pile of silk cushions
Off stage—Shackles and a chain (DICK, CICELY and CAT)
Personal—Whistle (MASTER OF THE HOUSEHOLD)

SCENE 2

Off stage—Sword (DICK)
           Sword (KING RAT)

74

Scene 4

Off stage—Bandages and a sling (King Rat)

Scene 6

Off stage—Sun helmet, cloak, suitcase (labelled) (Cicely)

Scene 7

Off stage—Basket of kittens (White Cat)

9 780573 064227